# ENTREPRENEURSHIP IS A BEAUTIFUL THING

*A Must Read for Aspiring and Seasoned Business Owners*

## YEMISI ADEYEYE

Copyrights: © 2020 Yemisi Adeyeye

Entrepreneurship Is A Beautiful Thing

www.yemisiadeyeye.com

**All rights reserved.**

This publication may not be reproduced, distributed, or transmitted in any form or by any means, including photocopying, recording, or other electronic, digital or mechanical methods, without the prior written permission of the publisher, except in the case of brief quotations embodied in critical reviews and certain other non-commercial uses permitted by copyright law.

The information in this book was correct as at the time of publication and according to various researches, but the author does not assume any liability for loss or damage caused by errors or omissions.

**Book Cover Design and Publishing:**

The Book Surgeons International - @thebooksurgeons
thebooksurgeons@gmail.com

+2349090885868, +2347061082014

www.thebooksurgeons.com

Malhub, House 6, Agba dam Link Road, GRA, Ilorin, Nigeria.

## Dedication

This book is dedicated to all women in entrepreneurship and the men who support us; most especially my husband and business partner, Dr Ademola Adeyeye. Your support made me a confident manager and a better leader.

# Acknowledgements

First, I appreciate and acknowledge God who gave me a new life after two weeks in a coma. He made this project possible and to Him be all the glory in Jesus Christ's name (Amen).

I acknowledge the immense support of my husband, Dr Ademola Adeyeye, for supporting and encouraging me while writing this book.

My heartfelt gratitude goes to my darlings, Princess Adesewa and King Adejolaoluwa, for giving me the time to achieve this. You are the reason I smile.

Also, I acknowledge the immense support of Lifefount Hospital and Foundation Team for making the management of a 24/7 business easy, organised, and profitable. You all gave me confidence to teach what I do.

I recognise the tremendous support and expertise of Mr Akolade Oluwatoba and his team, who pushed me till my concept became a product.

To Mr Samuel Farohunbi, Mr Gabriel Ochehepo, Dr Dolapo Amusan, and Mr Ken Kamaldeen, my deepest gratitude goes to you for giving me the IT support at different times and helping me gain online credibility and visibility.

Moreover, I give admiration and gratitude to my mentors and coaches. Learning from you changed my life positively.

Finally, my sincere appreciation goes to my mentees for their thirst for knowledge, which drives me to do more; and to my family, friends and followers, you are my blessings.

'Entrepreneurship involves using systems and strategies with limited resources to create values and provide solutions (products or services) to problems while taking associated risks and gaining profits.'

— *Yemisi Adeyeye.*

# Foreword

It is a great honour and privilege for me to write the foreword of this great book. I met Dr Yemisi Adeyeye in 2016 when I went to train a class of female entrepreneurs in Abuja, Nigeria, on Financial Management. In a class of almost fifty participants, she stood out by her participation in and after class interactions. That was the beginning of our relationship.

My curiosity was that I had never met a medical doctor who was so passionate about entrepreneurship. She is a medical doctor who started (with her husband) Lifefount Hospital with extensive practical experience of managing and running a successful business and foundation that empowers both aspiring and existing entrepreneurs.

Dr Adeyeye once said in one of her business summits, 'there is the art and act of running a business'. When I heard this, I knew there was a book in her waiting to be birthed. Today, I am excited that this has finally come to reality.

There are plenty of books on the practical aspects of setting up your own venture—from registering your business to recruiting your staff, etc., but this book is more than that. Businesses don't succeed or fail based on whether you register or not. This book is about the spirit of entrepreneurship—the essentials that differentiate successful entrepreneurs from struggling entrepreneurs. It demystifies entrepreneurship and gives practical steps to help you build a lasting and thriving business.

By writing this business manual, Dr Yemisi Adeyeye has simplified and presented the ingredients to successful entrepreneurship based on timeless and universal principles applicable anywhere in the world. This is a product of painstaking research on the requirements of successful entrepreneurship, aided by years of practical experience of managing and running a successful hospital and foundation. It is a harvest of years of empowering and building young entrepreneurs.

Perhaps you don't have an idea for a business, but you know you want to start out on your own. That's fine; this book will help you find the right concept for your business. You may have the idea already but don't know how to grow it into a full-blown business, or you have already started your business and you want to take it to the next level. You might even be a thriving entrepreneur already, but you realise there are some missing puzzles and you want to be better. Wherever you are on your entrepreneurship journey, this book will help you raise your game and become better.

Simply grab your pen and notepad and start reading this book to discover how to become a more successful entrepreneur. I wish you all the best as you practise and apply all you'll learn in this book.

**Abimbola Osuchukwu.**
CEO, Valucon Business Services.
@bimpreneur

# Contents

Dedication — iii

Acknowledgements — iv

Foreword — vii

Introduction — 1

Chapter One: Fundamentals Of Entrepreneurship — 3

Chapter Two: Yemisi Adeyeye's Entrepreneurship Model — 11

Chapter Three: Attributes Of A Highly Successful Entrepreneur — 35

Chapter Four: Legal Business Entities: Give Your Business A Name — 52

Chapter Five: Vision, Mission, And Corporate Governance — 63

Chapter Six: Human Resources

| | Management | 99 |
|---|---|---|
| Chapter Seven: | Marketing: The Seven Steps To Making Huge Sales And Gaining Brand Loyalty | 117 |
| Chapter Eight: | Customer Relationship Management | 151 |
| Chapter Nine: | Business Plan | 189 |
| Chapter Ten: | Mind Your Finances: Bookkeeping And Accounting Principles | 214 |
| Chapter Eleven: | Mind Your Finances: Classification Of Account | 241 |
| Chapter Twelve: | Mind Your Finances: Taxes | 273 |
| Conclusion | | 289 |

# Introduction

This book, *Entrepreneurship Is A Beautiful Thing,* is a guide on how to structure and grow your business so that it can be successful, sustainable, and also outlive you.

It focuses on the fundamentals of entrepreneurship and arms you with skills that will transform your business to an organisation that can run with or without your active supervision.

It is spiced with stories of the author's experiences on her entrepreneurial journey and her learning from different institutions, organisations, networks, and mentors.

Reading this book will add immense values to you and your business which includes:

- Staff management skills using policies,

processes, and standard operating procedures.

- Understanding financial laws and acts that guide enterprise management.

- Understanding the basics of bookkeeping, accounting, and marketing for Micro, Small, and Medium Enterprises Sector (MSME).

- Gaining more confidence in delegating duties that relate to business operations and focusing on your business management.

- Boosting your corporate governance skills and making your business ready for investment and many other opportunities available to MSME Sector.

- Earning quality time for family and other things you have a passion for, without worrying about the business crashing in your absence.

## Chapter One

# FUNDAMENTALS OF ENTREPRENEURSHIP

Entrepreneurship is not only about buying and selling or rendering a service. It's about knowing the art and proper management of a business. Daily business owners are saddled with the responsibility of rendering services, manufacturing, or distributing products. Business owners find their businesses falling apart due to a lack of business management skills. However, businesses have huge potentials to grow when corporate governance is in place. To understand business management, let's look at the concept of entrepreneurship.

Entrepreneurship has its origin from the French word *entreprendre* which means *to undertake or start a thing*. An entrepreneur is somebody who undertakes a particular business pathway or starts a business. That is why some are called founders and co-founders.

Entrepreneurship is now commonly used, but it has different meanings to different individuals. If a hundred people are asked to define it, each person will have something to say based on his perspective. Some will define it by their experiences or observations.

Some may say it is the acquisition of skills or an act of buying and selling. Others may say it is an act that brings money to one's pocket. Each definition is correct but there is more to entrepreneurship than those meanings.

Other words that can be used to describe entrepreneurship include business, venture capital, enterprise creation, firm formation, corporate, company, start-up, pioneering, industrialism, and trade.

Professor Howard Stevenson of Harvard Business School is regarded as the Godfather of entrepreneurship. He defined entrepreneurship as the process of pursuing opportunity beyond resources under one's control.

Wikipedia referred to entrepreneurship as designing, launching, and running a new business.

While writing this book, I thought about so many things and came up with my opinion on the definition of entrepreneurship. From my experiences, I can define entrepreneurship as the process of using systems and strategies with limited resources to create values and provide solutions (products or services) to problems while taking associated risks and gaining profits.

This means that there is a pursuit of opportunity (values) that should not be hindered by the limited resources you have. In it, you are expected to go beyond those resources by using systems (policies, processes, and procedures) to make something (solutions) out of what you have, to solve problems.

As a trained medical doctor, I co-founded Lifefount Hospital with my business partner, who is a brilliant medical doctor and surgeon. I thought we had all it takes to run a hospital as a profitable enterprise, as we were full of excitement about creating solutions in form of qualitative healthcare services for our clients.

We were, however, shocked to discover that all we knew were the technical and operational aspects of our business, but not training and experience in business management skills. We started with two employees but noticed that there were many aspects of business management we knew nothing about. Taxes and so many other unforeseen issues also arose.

We had two choices: to learn entrepreneurship and grow or to continue without business knowledge and be stagnant or fail. My business partner and co-founder focused on the operational aspect while I shifted attention to enterprise management. This led to my executive certifications in entrepreneurial management at Enterprise Development Centre (Lagos Business School) of the Pan-Atlantic University, Nigeria and in Leadership and Management in Health at the University of Washington.

I also participated in many other entrepreneurship programs like Africa's Management Initiative, Cherie Blair Foundation, Tony Elumelu Foundation, and Academy for Women Entrepreneurs of Public Affairs Department of USA embassy in Nigeria.

These opportunities in business education deepened my knowledge of enterprise management and improved my corporate governance skills. I moved from ignorance to knowledge in entrepreneurial management. Consequently, I experience peace of mind and business growth by practising what I learnt.

My passion for teaching entrepreneurship and helping others grow increased daily. I have been fortunate to stand on different platforms, both nationally and internationally, to teach what I practise.

I believe that when aspiring and seasoned business owners are armed with the right knowledge, they will manage their businesses and turn them into organisations that can run effectively with or without their active supervision. They will also be able to build companies that can outlive them like some global brands that have thrived for many generations, today.

Your business should bring you joy and peace of mind but that is not many business owners' experiences, today. The majority experience pain and heartaches. They can only call themselves self-employed but cannot take a break or a vacation because their businesses depend totally on them.

Their businesses have no documented policies, processes, and procedures in place to guide actions and tasks in their establishments; and every decision-making step needs their actions, constant presence, and approval. If you are in this category, do not worry; know that this book will guide you in turning your hustle (like some people call disorganised business) into an organisation.

I wrote this book to guide you into becoming the Chief Executive Officer (CEO) you have been dreaming of. I discovered that I have had so much peace since I introduced systems into my business and that is what I have planned for you.

Business is war but using the right systems can make it peaceful.

This will bring me to what I call **Yemisi Adeyeye's Entrepreneurship Model.**

This model will help you understand entrepreneurship, its processes, systems, and rewards. With it, you will have confidence as a CEO and leave the company of those who lack peace of mind and don't know what to do or who to turn to, for help in their entrepreneurship journey.

**Yemisi Adeyeye's Entrepreneurship Model** will also help aspiring business owners to understand and start entrepreneurship rightly. I will discuss this in detail in the next chapter.

'Business is war but the use of the right systems in your business is peace!'

*-Yemisi Adeyeye*

## Chapter Two

# YEMISI ADEYEYE'S ENTREPRENEURSHIP MODEL

Yemisi Adeyeye's Entrepreneurship Model is a model that explains entrepreneurship. It uses *Four-Colour Coded Quadrant* to explain the process of using systems and limited resources to create solutions to identified problems and stress the benefits of entrepreneurship and the entrepreneur's 4Cs: CEO, Company's Staffs/Employees, Clients, and Community.

In this model, I explained four different aspects of entrepreneurship as embodied in the definition I gave in the previous chapter.

The first quadrant is the Problem (Red) Quadrant, the second is the Solution (Yellow) Quadrant, the third is the System (Green) Quadrant, while the fourth quadrant is the Benefit (Purple) Quadrant.

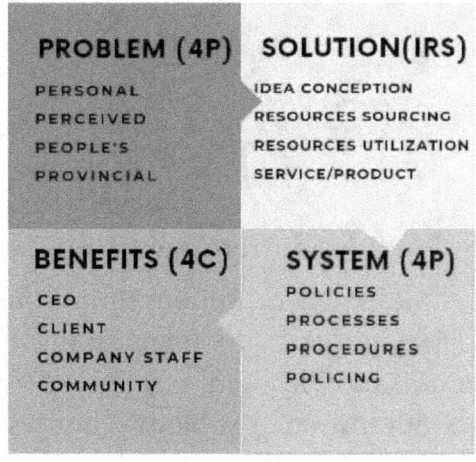

YEMISI ADEYEYE'S ENTREPRENEURSHIP MODEL

By using traffic light colour codes, you can sense what I'm trying to drive at. It is common knowledge that in traffic lights, *Red* means *To Stop*, *Yellow* means *To Get Ready* (an improvement over the red), and *Green* means *To Go* (productivity, fruitfulness, and increase which means that you are in a good place).

Including Purple is deliberate as it stands for royalty, where the benefit of entrepreneurship sits. Most small businesses, however, are in the yellow zone. You need to ask yourself these questions: where is my business? Is it in the yellow, green, or purple zone? Am I getting benefits from this business and will it last for a long term in the purple zone?

Yemisi Adeyeye's Entrepreneurship Model's *four* quadrants are:

1) Problem Quadrant
2) Solution Quadrant
3) System Quadrant
4) Benefit Quadrant

## Problem/Red Quadrant

This quadrant can be divided into *four* levels which are: personal, peoples', perceived, and provincial problems.

- **Personal Problems**

    A problem you want to solve could be personal, but you know others have such challenges as well. You know that solving such a problem for yourself will allow you to commercialise the solution for others who have similar problems.

    My husband and I moved to a new environment in 2009 during my first pregnancy, when the delivery date was near. The excitement of a new house and a new baby on the way were so real that I did not notice the next viable hospital, in case of any emergency, was distant from our new home.

    After moving in, I discovered I would need help in getting to the hospital since emergency medical services/paramedics agencies were not active at my location.

    It won't be a pleasant story to tell that a doctor delivered a baby in an unpleasant situation or place without medical help, since my husband was a surgeon-in-training on many night calls in the hospital.

    I also noticed that some neighbours

showed up for health advices in our home and this pointed to the need for a healthcare centre in the community. Immediately I identified the problem of a lack of hospital in the neighbourhood, it sparked the idea of starting Lifefount Hospital.

What are the challenges you are going through? Maybe God is pointing your mind towards the solution you should provide for yourself and commercialise for others.

In my first year in clinical school, I noticed I could not get hot meals in the school area while studying at night, so I resorted to taking cold drinks and pastries whenever I was hungry. Students needed healthy, hot meals as dinner while reading in school at night; but the need I had was money.

My parents, Late Elder Kunle and Mrs Bisi Lawrence, were civil servants with many responsibilities. They paid my school fees and met some basic needs but left some other needs unmet. As a young, beautiful lady, I chose not to take any wrong step in sorting out my challenges.

I was engaged to my fiancé who gave me financial support from his meager pay as an intern in a missionary hospital in Ogbomoso, Western Nigeria. Despite the support, I still found myself in a lack of money sometimes, which affected my focus during my undergraduate years. This personal problem got me thinking of ways to solve it.

- **Peoples' Problems**

You can start a business by identifying other peoples' problems, although, you may not experience them at all. For example, if you live in an area where public transportation does not exist and you can only give a ride to only four people in your car, you can start a transportation and logistics business from the problem you see others go through. Most solutions that come from the foundation of solving a particular problem usually do well.

- **Perceived Problems**

Identifying problems is fundamental to creating solutions. We can perceive future problems and sometimes with great insight, we see into the future that a problem will arise and we need to get set to tackle it.

Another way you can see the problem is to

perceive it. It is called a *perceived problem*. For example, COVID-19 started in Wuhan in 2019, and it was predicted that it would spread. The pandemic didn't spread to Africa until 2020 and some people knew there would be a need for protective wears which they ordered from China before all borders were shut.

Can you see how a perceived problem can be something you want to solve?

- **Provincial Problems**

The problem you want to solve may be peculiar to an area, a province, or a sector of life. Those who see problems first, usually do well in forming unique ideas that will solve them. Do **not** create a solution before looking for problems it can solve.

If you are about to start your business, consider the Red Quadrant very well. A business that will last will start by identifying a problem through any of the *four Ps* listed above.

Sometimes, people complain that the market is saturated with a particular type of business and wonder how to play in such a market. If this sounds like you, do not worry;

because it is possible.

I usually advise that instead of starting the same business, populating the market, and struggling for customers, you can study the industry and identify the challenges they face; then come up with fantastic ideas turning your would-be competitors into your customers.

Lifefount Hospital identified the need for endoscopy services in our vicinity, and so added it to our services. This makes us relevant even to our competitors who need endoscopy for their patients as they refer them to us. We have, therefore, turned from being competitors to collaborators.

Identifying problems in an industry or a business sector helps you to create solutions that your competitors will also patronise. Don't start a business because others are doing it. In most cases, it ends in heartache.

Do you see any need around you?

The need you will identify may be in another person's business.

Can you render a service or create products

to solve them?

If you want to do a business that will make you money and earn you appreciation from your clients, look for problems around you and solve them.

### Solution/Yellow Quadrant

After identifying a problem, the next thing is to conceive ideas on how to solve them.

Entrepreneurs are meant to *provide solutions,* but to provide a solution fit for the market, you need to find out and answer the following questions appropriately:

- What are the needs identified?

- Who are those having these identified problems?

- Is the identified problem seen as a problem by those you intend to sell to? Sometimes you see something as a problem, but those involved may not see it as a problem. This can make selling solutions to them difficult.

- Are they willing to buy your product or service?

- How much are they willing to pay?

This will help you know the cost that must go into your production or service so you don't have a product that buyers cannot afford.

All these questions are part of your market research and they will help your decisions in conceiving solution ideas, sourcing and utilising resources during production, and while rendering your services.

The solution quadrant works with the acronym: IRRS.

- Idea conception
- Resources sourcing
- Resources utilising service/Product creation
- Services/Products

After identifying a problem and deciding to provide solutions to it, you need to move to the next phase: idea conception. Simply ask yourself this critical question: what are the resources I need, to create solutions to those problems? Afterwards, make a list of the resources needed and then source for them. Your level of sourcing for resources depends on the solutions you intend to provide.

The resources needed to start an enterprise include:

- Financial Resources (Funding)
- Human Resources (Employees)
- Educational Resources (Industrial Know-how)
- Physical Resources (Premises and Equipment)
- Emotional Resources (Support Systems)

For those who are into Information Technology (IT) solutions, the resources will be virtual resources on the internet.

The size of the resources needed also depends on how big you want to start. I usually tell entrepreneurs that it is better to start small and grow their enterprise than to start big (without prior experience and validation of idea) and fail.

We started Lifefount Hospital as a small clinic with two employees and at that point, many unexpected issues came up, but at a small scale, which we dealt with successfully without relenting.

Several times, resources are limited, but it is the responsibility of an entrepreneur to think out of the box and provide solutions to the identified problems. An entrepreneur must maximise available limited resources and utilise them to create products or services.

### System/Green Quadrant

Many business owners are making sales in their businesses, but they desire more than just sales that depend solely on their active involvement in the business. They desire a sustainable enterprise that can run smoothly and profitably without their active supervision. This is where I want you, my dear reader, to be.

In the *Green Quadrant*, you will have peace of mind, sustainability, and you can take a vacation, open branches or even franchise your business.

Many business owners are just self-employed. They are in charge of the daily operational activities of their company. Although, it is okay for a business owner to understand the nitty-gritty (the essence or core) of a business operation.

For example, in a soap-making business, the

entrepreneur can understand the soap-making process but if making the soap is all he does every day, he will not be able to perform the functions of the chief executive officer and give strategic leadership to the enterprise.

Entrepreneurship means doing business in an organised way. Yemisi Adeyeye's Entrepreneurship Model explains that entrepreneurship involves sourcing, organising, and utilising resources to make products or services; and to achieve a sustainable enterprise, you must introduce systems into it. I believe this is the most tasking and rewarding part of entrepreneurship.

Entrepreneurship is what makes your business an organisation, not only where you make money and keep being busy all year round; but an organisation positioned to solve problems for a long time without giving headaches to the owner.

System Quadrant has *four Ps* guiding its principles, which are:

- Policies
- Processes
- Procedures, and
- Policing.

A lasting business must have systems and structures in place, with documented processes and policies. The system is the most important part and it is where entrepreneurship sits.

The reason business owners usually lose opportunities is because their setups do not have working systems. Business owners must train their employees on how to deliver the operational aspect of the business excellently, so they can focus on the business management as the CEO.

A business that will grow exponentially needs strategic planning, direction, and leadership. Combining management with the core operational tasks of a business is not easy to do. Oftentimes, the management aspect suffers and the company's growth decreases.

To give your company wings to fly is to focus on its management and ensure you put the right *policies*, *processes*, and *procedures* in place while paying attention to control measures described as *policing*.

- **Policies**

A policy is a documented principle of behaviour and conduct thought to be desirable or necessary, especially as formally expressed by a government or other authoritative body. It is the art of governance.

Dear business owner, you need to have the principle of conduct in your enterprise. This guides everyone, including yourself, on how to behave in different situations and strengthens the capacity of those who assist you in co-ordinating others like your managers and Heads of Departments. They will know how to handle situations without waiting for your opinion every time.

- **Processes**

A process is a series of events or tasks which produces a result in an enterprise. Workflows must be carefully thought through and documented before you can get results.

Your team, which comprises your managers or employees, must understand how to navigate between a task and another to achieve desirable results within the various departments. For example, you need to document the several stages of the hiring process of your Human Resources (HR) Management Department so that whoever is in charge of HR afterwards will follow and achieve the same result at the end of the process.

- **Procedures**

A procedure is also known as Standard Operating Procedures (SOPs). Standard Operating Procedures are a set of specific guidelines, rules, and regulations (sometimes mandated by some regulatory boards) a company needs to follow to achieve a task or set goals.

SOPs are methods for performing a task. They are documented guides that state the step-by-step instructions on a particular task. An organisation must have SOPs for different tasks so that the employees can follow them religiously to achieve great results always. SOPs are like a cookbook; every time you follow the recipe strictly, you will get the same menu with the same great taste, irrespective of who does the cooking.

Business owners need to document their company's policies, processes, and procedures so their employees can have access to it always. They can hire the service of HR/business consultants to help them with producing tailor-made policies for their companies, which will help achieve the desirable companies' cultures. Managers or Heads of Departments (HODs) coupled with the supervision of business owners, can help to create and document the company's policies.

- **Policing**

Police are a body of officers representing the civil authority of government. They maintain public order and safety, enforce the law, prevent, detect, and investigate criminal activities. These functions which they perform are known as policing.

Policing means that there should be control and regulation in whatever you are doing just like a country's police enforces the law, creates order, and punishes people who are not doing the right thing. That is what you should do in your business. As the CEO of bigger businesses, you cannot do it alone as you will depend on your unit heads or the HR department to do policing for your company.

You must be ready to support and get the agreement of your team members on the policy creation to ensure everyone is on board.

Compliance is easier when your team members or employees understand the policies and embrace them as a tool for correction.

Dear business owners, as you make great company policies, add sanctions for defaulters, too.

Create control measures to ensure that everyone follows the instructions fully. Reward those who comply and sanction defaulters. These can be done when you put the right controls in place.

I developed the ultimate company policy manual templates which help business owners to create their customised company's policies easily and pave way for structured enterprise and peace of mind.

### Benefit/Purple Quadrant

This last quadrant explains the beauty of entrepreneurship. It is the quadrant of reward. Your business will provide benefits to you and others once the right strategies are put in place.

The purple quadrant describes the *four Cs* of benefit. It will benefit the:

- CEO
- Client
- Company
- Community

### CEO's Benefits

When you start a new business, it's like giving

birth to a new baby; it requires a lot of attention and nutrition to grow.

Your business requires funding and all the attention it can get for it to grow. In your business's growth, you may encounter some risks. The risks are inevitable, but you must not give up until you see growth. You must not allow the challenges of entrepreneurship to discourage you. The challenges you may face are:

(a) Finances

The financial resources needed to start and grow a business can be expensive, but if things don't go well, you may face substantial financial loss. In addition, you'll have no guaranteed income.

(b) Stress from worrying about competition, employees, bills, equipment breakdowns, and customer problems.

(c) Time commitment as you may have less free time compared to when you work for another person.

(d) Undesirable duties

You'll be responsible for overseeing everything

that needs to be done, and you'll probably have to perform some unpleasant tasks like firing people.

If you do not give up because of these challenges, you will enjoy the benefits of entrepreneurship.

That profit may not come in the first few years, but as you introduce the right strategies and systems with great management, growth is certain.

As the CEO of a business, you have lots of benefits which include:

- Independence, since you are your boss.

- Ability to decide when and where you want to work and create a lifestyle for yourself because you're in charge.

- Involvement in all aspects of your business and acquiring learning opportunities.

- Ability to work in a field you enjoy because you will have creative freedom and personal satisfaction from watching your business succeed.

When you run your business, you get a chance to make more money than when an employer employs you. Owning your business is a sure pathway to financial freedom and rewards.

## Clients' Benefits

Your solution is what your clients are interested in and very happy with, because they are getting solutions to their problems.

Customers get a good feeling of satisfaction from using your solution. The innovation and thoughtfulness clients see in your business from using your products or engaging your services give them satisfaction.

Customers' needs are dynamic and business owners must be on top of their game to continue to give huge benefits to their customers. These kinds of services increase customer's pride and boost their loyalty.

## Company's Staffs/Employees' Benefits

Your business is not only beneficial to you and your customers but also your employees.

Employees get paid their wages or salaries which are compensations for the work done. Having a paid employment boosts their morale and a warm and conducive work environment is beneficial to the emotional well-being of your staff.

Depending on the laws guiding businesses in an area the business is situated, there are different added benefits to the employees which include, but are not limited, to unemployment insurance, health insurance, annual and medical leave, housing insurance, and other support.

Dear business owner, whatever challenges you go through while running your business, do not give up because many people depend on the benefits from your business more than you know.

### Community's Benefit

Enterprises create jobs and reduce unemployment in the nation. As a business owner, the community benefits from your enterprise either directly or indirectly. The community can be your immediate environment, the nation, or even the world at large. Your business gives people in the community a sense of pride. When youths are gainfully employed, they contribute to nation-building and neither involve themselves in criminal activities nor become restive.

Government-controlled systems, like healthcare and education, depend on individual and company's taxes. Lifefount Hospital that started many years ago as a mini-clinic from an apartment in the city's outskirt has grown to be one of the leading private hospitals in the city providing cancer treatment, major surgeries, endoscopies, maternal and child care services, and rendering value as a referral centre for other hospitals in Nigeria.

Know that your effort in building a formidable business is beneficial to you, your clients, employees, and everybody.

Entrepreneurship is about running an organised business and scalability is possible when your business is organised.

'Entrepreneurship is about running an organized business.'

*-Yemisi Adeyeye*

## Chapter Three

# ATTRIBUTES OF A HIGHLY SUCCESSFUL ENTREPRENEUR

The Green Quadrant in the *Yemisi Adeyeye's entrepreneurship* model is very vital in building a sustainable enterprise that will thrive for a long time.

Some folks are privileged to start a business with most of the resources they require. Others have access to a very limited resources for initiating their dream businesses. Whatever category you belong, please know that you already have the most important resources you need. On the foundation of this resource, you can build and gain all other resources.

That most important resource you have or need is *you*. No one is born empty. You are worth it and your dreams are valid.

An entrepreneur is an individual who creates a new business, bears most of the risks, and enjoys most of the rewards. Entrepreneurs who prove to be successful in taking on the risks of a start-up are rewarded with profits, fame, and continuous growth opportunities.

Entrepreneurship is an important driver of economic growth and innovation. An entrepreneur combines resources to manufacture goods or to provide services for his customers. He creates a business plan, hires labour, acquires resources and financing, and provides leadership and management for his business. He commonly faces many obstacles like hiring talents, getting finances, and overcoming bureaucracy when building the company. A highly successful entrepreneur must have some attributes that will help in overcoming the obstacles and challenges in his pathway towards building his dream organisation.

Highly successful entrepreneurs possess some of the following qualities stated below, and much more. If you search within yourself and discover a lack in any of them, you can build yourself in those areas and also ensure your team members complement you.

Everyone has the potential of becoming highly successful entrepreneurs. However, there are a few key personality traits that successful entrepreneurs have in common. These include:

**(a) Creativity**

Creative thinking helps entrepreneurs to produce unique business ideas. Successful entrepreneurs are creative while thinking. They think critically and creatively in order to create unique solutions to problems. They also think outside the box and, most times, think like there is no box.

The wild creativities of many company creators make them thrive. Entrepreneurs are forced to come up with original ideas that differentiate their companies from others in the face of stiff competition.

**(b) Passion**

An entrepreneur must display a passion for his product, service, team, and business. His passion must be clear in the way he talks and acts. Successful entrepreneurs have strong feelings towards their vision, and they can't be easily dissuaded from their goals.

It takes passion to feel motivated enough to keep moving on in business despite all challenges. Highly successful entrepreneurs are successful because they choose to do what they love.

### (c) Robust Work Ethics

Highly successful entrepreneurs are not lazy. They are always hardworking and sometimes more than others. They are usually the first to arrive at the office and sometimes, the last to leave and they work till projects are complete.

### (d) Motivation

Entrepreneurs are highly motivated people. They will put in the long hours in order to start and sustain their enterprise. They also work and strive towards a defined goal in anticipation of a fruitful outcome.

Highly successful entrepreneurs are people who do what needs to be done without being asked or encouraged to do so. They are always motivated to take initiative on their projects and be their own lead. When things get hard, a highly successful entrepreneur is challenged to grow and strengthen the business.

### (e) Optimism

Entrepreneurs do not look at the negative sides, but always see the positive and forge ahead in every situation. They are always expecting the best in all ways.

### (f) Future focus

Entrepreneurs always look towards achieving their goals by keeping their eyes on the future's picture. Their strong vision propels them and they are good listeners of ideas that will lead to the desired future and make them accountable and committed to their future.

### (g) Persuasion

Successful entrepreneurs know their businesses well; they can get people to listen and thoroughly convince them to take an interest in their big ideas and invest in them. They convince talents to work on their team or get people to buy their products or service.

You will require great storytelling skills to get money from investors, to build a great team, fund the start-up, recruit the best talent and advisors, and also in selling to customers.

### (h) Flexibility

Entrepreneurs must be able to switch roles as they cannot afford to employ all the employees they need at the beginning. While writing this chapter, I could remember that we could not afford all the employees needed on a shift at the inception of Lifefount Hospital, therefore, I used to do some duties to assist the nurse on duty to ensure we leave no task undone and at the same time, switching roles between being the team leader to being a team member.

Entrepreneurs must also know how to delegate to trained members of their team. As much as you want to do most tasks by yourself, the ability to delegate empowers your team members.

### (i) Resourcefulness

An entrepreneur must be resourceful. He must know how to maximise resources to achieve the set goals. As an entrepreneur, your business revolves around solving problems. In achieving this, you will encounter several challenges, including limited resources. Therefore, you must be able to find innovative ways to overcome these potential obstacles. You must maximise the resources, no matter how small, at your disposal. Also, you need to teach patiently and lead tactically.

### (j) Adventurous

The biggest risk you can take is not taking risk. Successful entrepreneurs are risk takers. We know them to plan for the unknown and make the best calculated decisions for their businesses. Many organisations were forced to work from home because of the global outbreak of coronavirus, resulting in many business owners making quick calculated decisions to stay afloat and survive. Entrepreneurs must possess an adventurous mind that is not rigid, but ready to move at a moment's notice in order to make things happen.

### (k) Decisiveness

Prompt decision making is a key attribute of an entrepreneur. There is no room for procrastination in business. As an entrepreneur, you must seize opportunities and get the job done.

### (l) Eagerness to Learn

An entrepreneur needs to learn all aspects of the trade, from customer relationship management to marketing, to accounting, and finally, bookkeeping. Many new businesses may not have all the required employees in every department due to lack of funding. Good entrepreneurs are always eager to learn, and this makes them very knowledgeable and well rounded. All their experiences are also learning opportunities.

Adopting these personality traits will indeed help you. Although you may possess many of these traits, they can always be fine-tuned and improved. If you lack any of these traits as an entrepreneur, try to ensure someone in your team has it and can complement your effort.

Having identified all these attributes, the next agenda is to ask yourself some soul-searching questions. Embarking on the entrepreneurial career path to *being your boss* can be exciting. But along with all your research, make sure to do your homework about yourself and your situation.

A few questions to ask yourself include the following:

What business should I start?

Do I have the personality, temperament, and mindset to take on the world on my terms? (Note that there are four main personality types and by doing a simple test, you can know which category you belong to. This will help harness your temperament into your style of leadership.)

Do I have the required ambiance and resources to devote all my time to my venture? (For those wanting to move from working for an organisation to becoming their boss, they must test the waters while still in paid employment. This will help ascertain if this new venture is profitable and able to pay the same salary or a significant fraction of it.)

Do I have an exit plan ready with a clearly-defined timeline in case my venture does not work?

Do I have a concrete plan for the next $x$-number of months or will I face challenges midway because of family, financial, or other commitments?

Do I have a mitigation plan for those challenges?

Do I have the required network to seek help and advice as needed?

Have I identified and built bridges with experienced mentors to learn from their expertise? ('Where no counsel is, the people fall; but in the multitude of counselors there is safety'- Proverbs 11:14 (NKJV). You can join entrepreneurial communities online such as the Lifefount Business Network Facebook group and many other amazing business groups or tribes to connect with experienced mentors.)

Have I prepared a complete risk assessment draft, including dependencies on external factors?

Have I realistically assessed the potential of my offering and how it will figure in the existing market?

If my offering is going to replace an existing product in the market, how will my competitors react?

To keep my offering secure, will it make sense to get a patent?

Can I wait that long?

Have I identified my target customer base for the initial phase?

Do I have scalability plans ready for larger markets?

Have I identified sales and distribution channels?

Does my entrepreneurial venture meet local regulations and laws? (This is very important so you don't run against the law.)

If not feasible locally, can I and should I relocate

to another region?

How long does it take to get the license or permissions from concerned authorities?

Can I survive that long?

Do I have a plan about getting the resources and skilled employees and have I made cost considerations for the same?

What are the tentative timelines for bringing the first prototype to market or for services to be operational?

Who are my primary customers?

What are the funding sources I may need to approach to make this big?

Is my venture good enough to convince potential stakeholders?

What technical infrastructure do I need?

Once I establish the business, will I have sufficient funds to get resources and take it to the next level?

Will other big firms copy my model and kill my operation?

In answering these questions, here are some of my personal guiding principles which will be useful:

There are many businesses you can start, but ensure it does not contravene the law of God and that of man.

Making money or hitting a huge profit should not be the only reason you embark on an entrepreneurial journey. For example, you cannot deal in drugs or human trafficking because it's against the Law of the Land and God's law.

When you commit your ways into God's hands, He will align it with HIS will. 'Commit your works to the LORD and your thoughts will be established'. (Proverbs 16:3 NKJV)

'For it is God who works in you to will and to act in order to fulfill his good purpose'. (Philippians 2:13 NIV)

That you desire to do a kind of business out of so many options in the world means that God must have planted the *will* in your heart. You will do well to involve Him in every step of the way, and He definitely will direct your path. Proverbs 3:5-6 NKJV says, 'Trust in the LORD with all your heart, and lean not on your own understanding; in all your ways acknowledge Him, And He shall direct your paths'.

1) Consider your natural tendencies (talent, passion, likes, and dislikes).

What are your talent, passion, likes, and dislikes? They could form the basis of your choice of business.

What talents do you have? Look inwards.

What are the things you do effortlessly and so well that people compliment you about? That may point to the solution you can turn into an enterprise.

Remember that one of the attributes of an entrepreneur is *being passionate*. Therefore, kindly answer this question: what are you passionate about?

Entrepreneurship is a lot of work in which you will need to depend on your passion to carry you through at some point when the going gets tough.

Do you have likes or dislikes? You can definitely build a business by solving the problems you dislike. A young man once told me how he disliked seeing trash heaped at a particular place in the city that he kept on talking of innovative ways to solve the public health issue. A solution to this issue came from his dislike.

2) Get the right counsel.

Before and during your entrepreneurship journey, seek counsel from business management consultants who have expertise in running an organised business. You can also get seasoned business owners, who have an enormous wealth of experience in managing organised businesses, to counsel or mentor you to be successful too. The Bible says, 'where there is no counsel, the people fall; but in the multitude of counselors, there is safety'. (Proverbs 11:14 NKJV). You will not have to make mistakes by yourself when you learn from other people's experiences.

3) Learn the ropes.

You can also get educated on the operational or the technical aspect of your business through internship, volunteering, or paid employment in that sector. Before starting Lifefount Hospital, I got a paid employment at a private hospital where they exposed me to managing a private healthcare business which gave me a huge confidence to co-found Lifefount Hospital, afterwards. Whenever or wherever you are learning the ropes, do not be there as a spy or to learn selfishly in order to run off and start your enterprise.

Give your best service and be loyal. When it is time to leave the setup, please disengage appropriately and leave it in a better state than you met it. Do your best to get your boss' endorsement because you may need it in the future.

Please note that there are many things you will learn by being in an environment or sector you wish to play in, through observation and active participation. At the young age of 11years, I used to assist my aunt, Mrs Adegboye, to run her bean pudding (moin-moin) business, and I learnt a lot about how to market my merchandise, which I have been using for my business. When you volunteer or serve others, you will pick up necessary virtues that will be useful in managing your own enterprise.

4) Research the field you are going into.

When starting from scratch, simply ask yourself these questions: what are the peculiarities in this geographical location I want to serve? Are my products or services needed in other places more than this location? If yes, how will I get my products to my prospective customers?

Should I move my business to a place where my potential customers are located? Is it cheaper to make my product here and transport to them? Should I consider availability of electricity before choosing my location? Should I consider affordable housing or rent for my business? Is security a factor to be considered before siting my business?

You should study the market you are going into so you can take over and dominate it. You can do a survey or questionnaire for your prospective customers, competitors, mentors, and the public to answer. Remember that the internet is a powerful resource to get many answers to your questions.

Asking and answering these relevant questions help in your business feasibility study and market research.

5) Start small and grow big.

Most great businesses started small. Samsung is a global brand now. The company makes a huge range of products from consumer electronics such as TVs, tablets, smart watches, virtual reality headsets, home theatre and audio, desktop computers, laptops, monitors, printers, and home appliances.

Who would believe that Samsung started

as a small, grocery trading company in 1938, trading and exporting goods produced in and around the city? It sold Korean fishes, vegetables, and noodles. As you start small solving indigenous problems, ensure you put global impact and relevance in view.

Your dreams are valid, dear entrepreneur. Seek knowledge, use it, and grow.

## Chapter Four

# LEGAL BUSINESS ENTITIES: GIVE YOUR BUSINESS A NAME

When you want to name your business, use unique names but shy away from names with offensive inclination. If your business is for a religious purpose, then a religious name may suffice; but if not, it may hinder clients who do not share your faith from patronising you.

It is okay to choose names that are easy to pronounce and remember. You may want to choose names with a global appeal rather than one which identifies only with a particular tribe. Please note that you should be free to name your enterprise and be ready to promote the name as you grow your business.

The relevant government agency in charge of business registration reserves the right to accept or reject a name if already taken or too similar to another entity. Do not harbour any hard feelings when facing rejections, rather, be innovative about the names you choose and try to register your entity.

In Nigeria, the Cooperate Affairs Commission (CAC) is in charge of company registration. You can personally access them online or use the services of a business registration consultant or a corporate lawyer.

The sector in which you want to deploy your business may reflect in your choice of name. For instance, Lifefount International Hospital is in the healthcare industry. This implies that such a business can only do hospital-related business activities and no business in other sectors, such as engineering.

The advantage is that from our name, you know the service we render and it's easy for you to refer health-care clients to us. There are some goods and services that enjoy some specific benefits. Using industry-specific names will give you access to such benefits. An example is with all health-care facilities which are exempted from paying Value Added Tax (VAT).

On the flip side, using a generic name may have its advantage as you will be able to do diverse businesses with such a name.

Now that you have named your business, you will now decide the kind of business entity you want to register.

### BUSINESS ENTITIES

An understanding of the different business entities that exist is important, so you can register the one that will help you achieve your goals. You also need to know the tax requirements of each entity so you can be prepared to run your business according to the laws that govern the entity from day one of your registration.

All business registrations start with a name search which you can do online, through a business registration consultant or a lawyer. A name can be rejected if already taken by another or too similar to another. As soon as a name is approved, it will be reserved for one month, after which it can be used by another entity if you do not register it on time.

Let's talk about the different types of entities and their characteristics. Different countries have their unique rules for business engagement. Please, find out what is obtainable in your country if your business is not in Nigeria.

## TYPES OF BUSINESS ENTITIES

- Business Name/Enterprise Registration/Sole Proprietorship.
- Partnership.
- Limited Liability Company (LLC).
- Limited by Guarantee.
- Not for Profit Organisation/Non-Governmental Organisations (NGO).
- Unlimited Liability Company (PLC).

### Business Name/Enterprise Registration/Sole Proprietorship and Partnership

This registration gives a legal structure to your business and it is the easiest and fastest to register. It can be registered by a single person who is 18 years and above or by multiple persons, as partnership.

It gives you an opportunity to do business with

people and some level of government, but the federal government and some corporation will only do business with Limited Liability Companies.

The liability of this registration can be transferred to the owners. This kind of business entity pays employees' taxes (Pay-As-You-Earn (PAYE)) monthly to the state revenue service on or before 10th of the following month, and Personal Income Tax (PIT) of directors annually to state internal revenue systems on or before March ending of the following year. I wrote on how to calculate PAYE and PIT in chapter 12.

Business name entities are to file their annual returns with the Corporate Affairs Commission. Always file all your certificates, receipts, and clearances, since you will have to refer to them sometimes. You are expected to audit your account annually. The 2020 financial act, however, gave some exemptions to small businesses.

Business name registration, either sole proprietorship or partnership, conveys liability to the business owners. That means if your company is liable but cannot pay your personal income, asset can offset the bill.

## Limited Liability Company

This registration is more expensive depending also on the shareholding in it. This entity takes a little longer to register, and approval requires due diligence.

A Limited Liability Company is a type of business structure where the company has a legal identity of its own, separate from its owners (shareholders) and managers (directors).

Limited Liability Company is a totally separate entity from the owners. It can sue and can be sued. Liability of this kind of entity is limited to its share capacity.

According to Wikipedia, *'limited by shares* means that the liability of the shareholders to creditors of the company is limited to the capital originally invested, i.e., the nominal value of the shares and any premium paid in return for the shares by the company. A shareholder's personal assets are thus protected in the company's event's insolvency, but any money invested in the company may be lost.

A limited company may be *private* or *public*. A private limited company's disclosure requirements are lighter, but its shares may not be offered to the public and therefore cannot be traded on a public stock exchange. This is the major difference between a private limited company and a public limited company. Most companies, particularly small companies, are private'.

Federal government and corporations only do business with or give contracts to this category of entity. If you desire to do business with big companies and the federal government, you would like to consider this kind of registration.

Please discuss thoroughly with your lawyer or business registration consultant so he can capture all your desired areas of business to prevent modification or re-registration when you want to expand your scope.

Limited companies are to file their monthly Value Added Tax report on or before the 5th of following month for the previous month, except small businesses with turnover less than twenty-five million are exempted. Failure to meet tax filing deadlines attracts sanctions.

As a business owner, your duty is to know these things so you can oversee your accountant, cashier, or staff to ensure there is no tax default as the burden of sanctions will be your sole responsibility. That is why you are reading this now.

Limited Liability Companies pays staff monthly PAYE and the directors pay annual Personal Income Tax (PIT) to the state revenue service.

Limited Liability Companies must get auditing firms to do annual external financial audit and pay their Company Income Tax (CIT) from profit made in the year under audit to the Federal Inland Revenue Service (FIRS). If your company is not in small business category but made a loss, you will file the losses.

The new financial act of 2020 has exempted companies with annual turnover of less than 25 million naira from company income tax (CIT).

There are some statutory payments irrespective of company loss or not. Such payments include; Education Tax, Social Trust Fund, and Industrial Trust Fund (ITF).

You will need the service of a Tax consultant to assist you in filing your taxes. They will advise you on the right things to do. I have worked with a few over the years and I will be willing to share their contacts with you upon request.

Some entrepreneurs claim loss or get exemption for the first 3 years, but some auditors advise against it as it prevents the company from the accurate analysis of its growth.

### Non-Governmental Organisations (NGO)

The non-profit organisation is registered for the sole purpose of solving societal issues. Those who practise this type of business do so to use the financial gains to solve a social problem. It is also a business model that puts the interests of people above all.

Whatever transactions are carried out is solely for the NGO's promotion. Founders are called trustees. The Board of Trustees (BOT) has a chairperson, a secretary, and one or more members. They direct the affairs of the NGO and can contribute to its growth but cannot share profit.

Those who work in an NGO are entitled to their salaries and will pay Pay-As-You-Earn (PAYE) but the Board of Trustees are not entitled to salaries.

NGOs are exempted from VAT and do not pay Company Income Tax (CIT), but they are required under the law to file VAT report, monthly, on or before 5th of the following month for the preceding month.

They will also file annual audited financials to Federal Inland Revenue Services (FIRS) and annual returns to Corporate Affairs Commission.

These laws are specific to countries, so find out what is obtainable in your country.

### Limited by Guarantee / Limited Social Enterprise

These are organisations that are owned by guarantors who agree to pay a certain amount of money towards company's debt. This type of company does not have stakeholders or shares.

Apart from the fact that share capital will not appear on the balance sheets, this type of organisation also pays tax, like a Limited Liability Company.

This business entity has a focus on a clause which allows it to give a percentage of its profit to a particular cause before deducting taxes. It has directors as guarantors who ensure that the company goes as directed in the article of registration. It comprises both limited companies and NGO and some call it *social enterprise*.

## Unlimited Liability Company

It is a liability company whose shares may be freely sold and traded to the public (although a PLC may also be privately held, often by another PLC), with a minimum share capital of #500,000 and usually with the letters PLC after its name. Similar companies in the United States are called Publicly-Traded Companies. Public limited companies will also have a separate legal identity.

Other variants of company registrations are available but not included on this list.

Please note that you will need a lawyer or business entity registration consultant to advice you and register your company. In some countries, registration is done online and can take between days to weeks.

## Chapter Five

# VISION, MISSION, AND CORPORATE GOVERNANCE

**VISION**

Every company must have a vision statement, which is a line stating where you see the enterprise in the future. A vision is a vivid mental image of where you want your business to be in the future, based on your goals and aspirations. Having a vision statement will give your business a clear focus and can stop you from heading towards the wrong direction.

The best way to formalise and communicate the

vision you have for your business is to write a vision statement.

A vision statement captures, in writing, the essence of where you want to take your business, and it can inspire you and your staff to reach your goals.

### What to Include in a Vision Statement.

A vision statement should communicate your long-term business goals, reflect your view of the world and your business's place in it.

It should also answer the fundamental question: *where are we going?* It usually deals with the practical aspect of *how will we get there?* in a mission statement or a business plan.

Certain aspects of your business may inspire your vision statement, such as finances (to sustain and support your family), reputation (among customers, staff, competitors), service quality standards (to make customers a priority), growth (you offer new products, innovate, get more customers, increase locations), passion (that you and your staff enjoy what you do), sustainability (that you are financially and environmentally sustainable).

You should also think about what inspired you

to start a business and what business values or principles are important to you.

## How to Write a Vision Statement

To write an effective vision statement, think about what your business does and imagine what it will look like, if it becomes the best possible version of itself. Writing a vision statement includes:

1. **Holding a Business Vision Workshop**

    A good first step in developing a vision statement is to invite your key staff to a business vision workshop. By brainstorming and sharing ideas, you can answer fundamental questions about the direction of your business, which will make it easier to write your vision statement.

2. **Documenting a Vision Statement**

    After holding your business vision workshop and coming up with some ideas, it's time to write your official vision statement. Usually, your vision is big, and it keeps propelling you forward. Your vision statement must:

- be clear and concise.
- be passionate, powerful, and memorable.
- be realistic according to your potential for growth and capacity.
- describe the ideal state of your company or best outcome.
- not use numeric measures of success.
- build a picture of what your future will be in people's minds.

Lifefount Hospital's vision is to be among the top five surgical centres in Africa, providing accessible medical care and reducing medical tourism outside our continent.

The bible says, '... Write the vision and make it plain on tablets, that he may run who reads it'. - Habakkuk 2:2 NKJV.

A company's vision differs from another, despite the similarities in businesses and operation in the same sector. A vision is a dream bigger than you and you will need to deploy a dynamic combination of resources and tact, at different times, to achieve it during your entrepreneurial journey.

## MISSION

A mission is the method your company will use to achieve its desired destination or vision. Lifefount Hospital's mission is to use cutting edge medical technology, exceptional customer service, and best professional practices in an aesthetic environment to achieve affordable and qualitative health-care.

Please note that the formation of company's mission and vision takes careful thought process for them to give direction to your enterprise. You can talk to a mentor or a business management consultant to achieve a robust, big, and global mindset vision and mission for your company.

Many start-up entrepreneurs cannot afford the services of a lawyer or other professionals, so I advise you to have friends across all boards, so you can leverage the power of networking and long-term friendship as you grow in life.

### Attributes of a Vision or Mission Statement

- Identifies clearly the corporate cultures, values, strategies, and view of the future.
- Addresses the effort every sector must put in place to achieve phenomenal results in the organisation.

- All statements must be actionable and what the company owners and staff/employees can do.
- A guide to management's thought pattern on strategic growth.
- Defines performance standards.
- Motivates staff and team to work with focus and enhance productivity.
- Educates customers, clients, investors, and competitors on what the enterprise is all about.

For the mission and vision statement to be properly executed, you need to educate all the members of your team, regularly and continuously, so they may understand and run with it. Remember to write and place this in an open place in your company for all to see.

## CORE VALUES

What are the values your company holds dearly and all staff must project at all times? What words summarise your company? Those are your core values. Our core values in Lifefount Hospital are Competence, Care, and Compassion (3Cs).

## COMPANY'S SLOGAN

Your slogan is when you or an outsider summarises your business in a sentence. It must be simple and speak the right message about your company. In Lifefount Hospital, our slogan is *extraordinary healthcare* because that's the experience we want to deliver to you once you contact our healthcare service.

## LOGOS AND COLOURS

Every company should have a logo which is a sign, pattern, design, or colour(s) that represents your company. You may design it yourself or let a professional graphic designer do it for you.

Ensure the logo is representing you exactly. Choose your colours wisely to represent you or your brand. In some places, getting some colours rightly when you print on paper and other materials may be difficult, so stick to primary colours.

When a professional graphic designer designed Lifefount Hospital's logo, its colour was *teal,* which is a mixture of *blue* and *green.* It looked like blue or green whenever we printed it, so from the beginning, we changed it to blue.

I really love Lifefount Hospital's logo. It's so beautiful and I am so proud of it. It represents our name well: *fountain of life.* There is a fountain. Red represents life and blue represents sound health. It's a very luxurious logo. Let your designer educate you on the colour codes for each colour so you can insist on the correct colour for your branding materials always.

Every colour has some other colour mixtures in it, so you can know the percentage present in each of your colour and ensure it stays the same, always. Ensure it represents your company. Do not copy other company's logo so you don't get sued.

In Nigeria, ministry of trades and investment handles trademark, therefore you can trademark your name and company's logos. Note, however, that you will have to use colours on your logo as your brand colour. Therefore, choose wisely and ensure you love your logo.

## CORPORATE GOVERNANCE

The company's executives are saddled with the daily operational management activities of a company, while the board of directors is saddled with a higher function of corporate governance. Directors can be executives or non-executives. As a business owner, you can be an executive director working in the company and doing operational management or only sit on the board as a non-executive director governing the company.

It is advisable to have independent non-executive board members who provide independent, non-biased opinions that help in governing the company.

For business entities who are sole proprietorships or partnerships, a board of advisors can provide similar functions as a board of directors, but majorly in an advisory position.

To develop your business, you need to leverage on the network, education, experience, and expertise of seasoned business owners and other professionals.

Corporate governance is a system of direction and control or rules, policies, and practices that dictates how a board of directors governs and oversees a company. It includes principles of transparency, accountability, and security.

Poor corporate governance can lead to a company's failure to achieve its stated goals. It can also lead to the company's collapse coupled with significant financial losses for shareholders, as highlighted by corporate finance Institute.

Many parties are directly or indirectly affected by your company's financial performance and they are interested in your company's corporate governance for different reasons.

These parties provide value to the corporation in the form of financial, physical, human, and other forms of capital. Interested parties include shareholders and stakeholders (directors, customers, etc.)

1) Shareholders
2) Directors, workers, and management receive salaries, benefits, and build reputation.
3) Investors expect to receive financial returns.
4) Lenders. This is based on specified interest payments, while returns to equity investors arise from dividend distributions or capital gains on their stock.
5) Customers are concerned with the certainty of the provision of goods and services with an appropriate quality.
6) Suppliers are concerned with compensation for their goods or services, and possible continuous trading relationships.

Good corporate governance gives confidence to shareholders and stakeholders to engage with your company, knowing that your company will deliver on their expected outcomes.

When corporate governance is not in place in

companies, shareholders and stakeholders are affected in many ways.

With bad corporate governance, the rights and fair treatments of shareholders become a mirage and the organisation's obligations to stakeholders, including employees, investors, creditors, suppliers, local communities, customers, and policy makers, cannot be carried out.

## THE FOUR P'S OF CORPORATE GOVERNANCE

Corporate governance is complex and those who have built their careers in fields where governance is a necessity might not fully understand everything it encompasses, but I will do my best to demystify it for small business owners.

I will break it down into four simple words: people, purpose, process, and performance.

These are the guiding philosophies behind the existence of governance.

- **People**

    The first $P$ is people. People are the founders or shareholders, the Boards of Directors, the stakeholders and consumers, and impartial observer.

- **Purpose**

    Every piece of governance exists for a purpose and the achievement of such purpose. What is your mission statement? Each of your policies and projects should exist to further company's agenda.

    The board meetings are to achieve company's agendas only. Boards and management meetings are geared towards making the business effective at achieving its stated purpose.

- **Process**

    Governance is the process by which people achieve their company's purpose, and that process is developed by analysing performances. Processes are refined over time to achieve a company's purpose, and it's always smart to employ a critical eye on your governance.

    You want to ask questions like:

    Can the processes be streamlined?

Can I efficiently achieve this purpose?

It takes work to make your processes function, but once they do, you will quickly see how they can help your company grow.

- **Performance**

Performance analysis is the core skill in any industry. The ability to look at the results of a process, determine whether it's successful, and then apply those findings to the rest of your organisation is one of the primary functions of the governing process. Therefore, use a critical eye on your governance to see if it's performing.

Don't forget that as a small business, you can leverage on your Board of Directors and/or Board of Advisors as sounding boards. You can discuss your ideas with them in order to get another opinion. That way, you won't think alone. With structures and systems in place, your venture is on a path to success.

The structures include:

- A functional organogram.

- Company's vision, mission, core values, slogan, and logo.

- Company's policies on different aspects like accounting, stock keeping, human resources management, marketing strategies, customers relationship policies, etc.

- A mindset that understands you are totally separate from your business and should be a good model to your staff.

During the first few years of establishing Lifefount Hospital, I thought we had everything needed for the business, but my thoughts were wrong as I discovered we knew a lot about treating human body but almost nothing about structuring the business. It is like many of us who are so good at making a product or providing a service but poor at the business of the product or service.

The knowledge gaps identified made us sought solutions which was a practical business education. These led me in many paths, including enrolling for entrepreneurial management programs at Enterprise Development Centre (Lagos Business School) which I could not afford as at then. I kept applying for different scholarships till I got a slot in the top 50 out of about three thousand applicants for Diamond Bank's (now Access Bank) Building Entrepreneurs Today (BET) program where I was rewarded with a 100% scholarship to study my desired program.

I also went through the Tony Elumelu Foundation's entrepreneurship program, Road to Growth program of the Cherie Blair foundation, African Managers' Initiative, and Academy for Women Entrepreneurs program of USA International Exchange Program.

These amazing programs gave me the education that covered my knowledge gap. My business partner and I have been able to govern our business and put structures in it, such that with or without our active involvement, the business can thrive. Also, mentoring others became easier since I have been leading by example.

As a business management consultant and a practising entrepreneur, people ask me severally: *what are the reasons businesses fail?* My answer always is: *businesses fail for many reasons; most especially due to lack of corporate governance. It is the responsibility of the small business owner to achieve good corporate governance.*

I want you to have it in mind that corporate governance comes with lots of advantages. When corporate governance is in place, business owners have peace of mind, and that's what this book brings to you.

A company must have the rules and policies that will govern the organisation. Hence, it becomes the company's culture as you adhere to it. You can hire a consultant to write this for you for a fee. You can use customised templates to suit your company's needs (see resources at: www.yemisiadeyeye.com), or write it yourself. Whatever you do, you must document your company's policies. Now it is obvious that the entrepreneur is the most important resource an enterprise needs. You are very valuable in building and governing the company you see in your vision.

One of your duties, as a business owner, is to ensure that your company has structure.

Thinking through your structure, what are your organisational and administrative structures? These will guide you on:

- The kind of people who will work with you (Job designations).

- The kind of job each person will do (Job description).

- How each task should be done (Standard

Operating Procedure (SOP)).

- How each position relates with others (Organogram).

- How each staff relates with the company (Company's policy).

If you cannot afford experts on these documents, as a business owner, you must do the documentation yourself.

You can check for relevant templates of documents online. This documentation will have the vision of the company's owner woven into it and that's what gives each company its originality. Many business owners want ready-made company policies. However, I make them understand that it's easy to download templates, but they will need to add their input so they can achieve their company's vision in order to build a unique brand.

Please note that the implementation of the documented policies is more important. Your company's policies must not just sit on the pages of your manual but must be a living document, the one you use actively, always.

Planning and documenting policies can be

stressful for some, but it's the pathway to having a company that can run on its own while you live an independent life, apart from your company. With the right systems in place, you can focus on management duties if you are an executive of the company or be on the board as a non-executive director and shareholder. Taking a vacation when necessary will be possible and you will find your company still standing and growing. This is the desire of every entrepreneur and it is achievable when you focus on management duties and not on daily operations or technical aspect of your business only.

With corporate governance it is easier to replicate the company in other locations, franchise, and to teach others how to do it.

Corporate governance makes it easy for other people and organisations to invest in your business, regardless of the stage and size. When a business is organised, who wouldn't want to be a part of it? Even if such business is not making profits yet, there is a tendency to make profits in the coming years. It will still attract investors.

Governing the financial aspect of your business is very important. To achieve this, take these tips very important:

1) You must have a separate bank account.

2) You must record all transactions in the appropriate account.

3) You must make budgets for spending. Budget helps you to know how much you will need to spend on each aspect of your business. All spending must be within budget. This prompts you not to make sales lower than you need to spend per time (monthly, quarterly, or yearly). Spending outside the budget requires deliberation and approval by your board/management.

4) Report monthly income and expenses. Ensure monthly requirement of the revenue service systems must be fulfilled. Please note their deadline dates and sanctions too. Nigerian Federal Inland Revenue Service (FIRS) and state Internal Revenue Service (IRS) are in charge of taxes. Federal Inland Revenue Service (FIRS) classified businesses into categories based on annual turnover.

The classifications include:

(a) Small enterprise (Less than twenty-five million naira turnover)

(b) Medium enterprise (Twenty-five million to

less than one hundred million naira turnover), and

(c) Large enterprise (Above one hundred million naira turnover). See details in chapter 12.

Businesses make annual returns to Corporate Affairs Commission (CAC) while external auditors make annual financial audit and reporting. CAC, however, is the body in charge of companies' registrations.

International Financial Reporting Standards (IFRS) is the best such that communicating your business with anyone, anywhere in the world, will be easy. The International Accounting Standards Board (IASB) issues IFRS, which in turn, sets common rules so that financial statements can be consistent, transparent, and comparable around the world. You can tell your auditor that you want your annual financial audit report to be IFRS compliant.

Your company's external auditors and tax consultants must advise you on fulfilling the appropriate financial obligations and taxes.

In Nigeria, financial obligations and taxes include:

a) **Nigeria Social Insurance Trust Fund (NSITF)**

The NSITF ensures the implementation of the

Employees Compensation Act (2010) which enables compensation in the event of death, injury, disease, or disability arising out of, or during employment. Employers have financial responsibility to NSTIF.

b) **Tertiary Education Tax (EDT)**

This is imposed on every Nigerian resident company at 2% of the assessable profit for each year of assessment. The tax is payable within two months of an assessment notice from the FIRS. Many companies pay the tax on a self-assessment basis along with their CIT.

c) **National Information Technology Development Levy (NITDL)**

This is for large and telecommunication companies.

d) **Capital Gains Tax (CGT)**

This is a levy charged on the positive difference between the sales price of an asset and the original purchase price. Capital Gains Tax is a flat rate of 10% of chargeable gains.

e) **Stamp Duties (SD)**

f) **Personal Income Taxes (PIT)**

Depending on the amount of chargeable income, the rate ranges from 7% to 24%. An individual whose income is less than N300,000 per annum is subject to a minimum tax of 1% gross income. See chapter 12 for how to calculate your tax or visit *www.yemisiadeyeye.com* to get a tax calculator.

In addition, you must file personal income tax returns on or before 31st March, annually; and remit your employees' PAYE (Pay As You Earn) every 10th day of the subsequent month.

For employers, you must remit and file taxes deducted from employees' income in the preceding year, not later than 31st January of every year for state revenue service audit. Therefore, you must keep all your tellers, receipts, and certificates, as you will need it again at the end of the year.

For an individual, failure to file PIT as and at when due attracts a fine of ₦5,000 and a sum of ₦100 for each day the default continues, or six months' imprisonment, or both. Similarly, a corporate body that fails to file a return on the due date will pay a fine of ₦500,000.

### g) Companies Income Taxes (CIT)

CIT is one of the major taxes collected by FIRS. Small businesses are exempted from CIT as stated in the financial act 2020. Please note that you must keep records to prove your exemption if asked to pay. CIT is a 30% tax charged on profits made by companies registered in Nigeria. This includes all the company's sources of income. Profits made from business activities outside Nigeria are exempted from paying CIT, as stated in the companies Income Tax Act (as amended).

According to the Act, you must pay CIT to FIRS not later than three months from the beginning of each year of assessment. A company is charged minimum tax when they make a loss, have no tax payable, or the tax payable is less than the minimum tax.

### h) Value Added Taxes (VAT)

Value Added Tax (VAT) is a consumption tax paid on purchased products or rendered services. Actually, the final consumer bears the burden of VAT. Unlike CIT, VAT is chargeable on goods produced both within and outside Nigeria. However, there are goods that are specifically exempted from VAT payment by the VAT Act. See list on VAT in chapter 12.

Usually, the standard rate for VAT is 7.5% but the new financial act exempted the small businesses from charging VAT.

Every taxable business owner is expected to file for their VAT monthly returns not later than 21st day following the month of transaction. Keep appropriate records to show you are in the exempted category in case you are asked to prove it.

## J) Withholding Taxes (WHT)

A withholding tax is an income tax paid to the government by the payer of the income rather than by the receiver of the income. WHT deductions are most times referred to as advance income payment. The rate for WHT ranges from 5% to 10% depending on the transaction.

WHT returns must be filed on the 21st day of every subsequent month. Failure to file on the due date attracts N25,000 for the first month of default and N5,000 for every other month the failure continues.

### K) Petroleum Profits Tax (PPT)

PPT is governed by Petroleum Profit Tax Act, Cap P13 LFN 2004 (as amended). It is levied on the income of companies involved in upstream petroleum operations. Another thing to note is that companies that pay petroleum income tax are exempted from paying Companies Income Tax on the same income.

### L) Pencom Obligation

A pension is a fund into which a sum of money is added during an employee's employment years and from which payments are drawn to support the person's retirement from work in the form of periodic payments.

A pension plan is a retirement account where employers and employees make monthly contributions. In Nigeria, the Pension Reform Act 2004 has a requirement for employers to contribute 10% of the salary and the employee contributes 8%—a defined contribution scheme. The employee receives the money when he retires.

Please note that these financial and tax obligations that concern your sector are mandatory if you want your business to grow and most especially if you want to do business with government, like getting contracts. Employers should ensure the consultants and employees responsible for carrying out these obligations do so in good time so as not to limit the organisational growth.

Corporate governance for a small business depends largely on the business owner. The following are my recommendations for small business owners:

Corporate governance makes it easier for people, organisations, and government to have confidence and trust to do business with you, notwithstanding your growth stage. If you are about to start or have started your company without writing rules, practices, and processes that will govern your enterprise, now is the time to take the necessary steps.

Corporate governance is also beneficial internally as it helps your employees to know that the management of the company is acting in the best interest of everyone. Corporate governance ensures policies are set and communication is given anytime there is a review.

The vision of the organisation must also be documented. Policies and procedures form the mode of the company's culture. The business owners or executive directors ensure everyone comports themselves in line with the vision and policies, thereby building the company's brand.

The duty of the CEO is to know his numbers (finances) and ensure strategic leadership of all aspects of the company. Business owners, however, must ensure monitoring and internal control of company's policies are in place, always.

Corporate Governance is essential in any organisation that desires to grow consistently. It ensures that adequate reporting system is put in place to provide accountability and transparency to the board and future investors. With corporate governance, it is not the business owner only who knows about the business. Some top employees too are aware since transparency is the order of an organisation.

Openness, disclosure, and accountability play a major role in contributing to business prosperity. Employers and employees are, however, governed by the company's policies.

## ORGANOGRAM

To build a great team, everyone must understand where they belong in the hierarchy of authority. An organogram makes this possible.

Organogram is a graphical representation of the flow of authority in your organisation. Those on top of the organogram include company owners, directors who own shares in your company, independent non-executive directors, and/or others who you've given the right to advice you (Board of Advisors).

Another name for organogram is organisational chart. It is a graphical representation of different relationships amongst functions, departments, teams, and individuals. It also goes further to mean a clear picture of command, flow of authority, and communication from the top to the bottom.

Organogram helps your team to know the line of command, who to relay to, and who to share feedback with. An organogram also shows the structure of an organisation, the relationships, and relative ranks of its part and position or jobs.

As a company's owner, please note that you have to be answerable to some others, either shareholders or stakeholders, so you can grow a sustainable business. You may be the alpha and omega of your business, but to grow well and build a business that will outlive you, you must be answerable to others, like directors, advisors, shareholders, and stakeholders. This is tough sometimes, but it's worth it in the long run.

*'If you want to go fast, go alone. If you want to go far, go together'* - African proverb.

Below is a sample of a simple organogram:

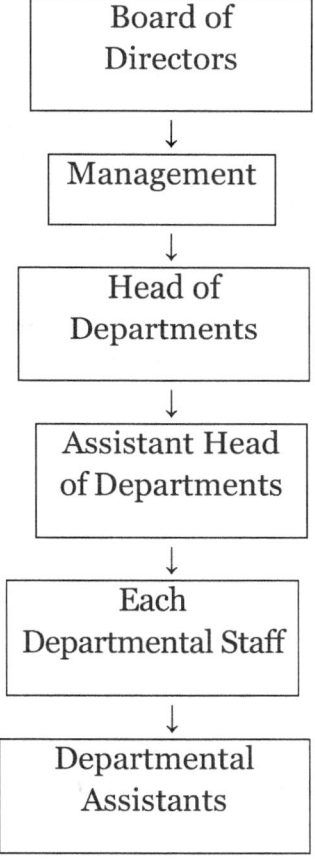

## JOB DESCRIPTIONS

Job descriptions are the documented roles and responsibilities attached to each designated position in the company. Each business owner should have this such that there will be clarity in what each person filling these posts must do, who they answer to, get to work with, or get feedback from. Please note that you can review and update these roles at intervals. Also note that you can employ a business development or HR consultant to do this for you, but you must provide them with details of what you want so their write up can represent your company well. These consultants can also help you with the hiring process for a fee if you don't want to do it by yourself.

## BOARD OF DIRECTORS

If you register your business as a business name, you will be referred to as a *proprietor*, but with limited registration, you and your partners can be called *directors*.

The board meet regularly in a year to give strategic direction to the organisation and the minute of the meetings are kept for follow-up and future references.

The Board of Directors is the registered shareholders of the business and it can comprise the executives or non-executives. The directors are usually the visionaries of the business. The board of directors is responsible for the legal and regulatory frame work, registration of the company, and ensuring the enterprise gets all necessary documentation, licenses, and opening of corporate bank accounts.

The board needs sufficient relevant skills and understanding to review and challenge management performance. It also needs adequate size and appropriate levels of independence and commitment.

Integrity, ethical behaviour, disclosure, and transparency are important attributes of members of the board. Organisations should clarify and make known the roles and responsibilities of board and management to provide clarity on their functions.

It is essential, however, that you make up a board of advisors as a small business owner, especially when your business is not a limited liability company. You need people of higher calibre who will use their expertise, education, experience, unbiased opinions, and their vast network to promote the growth of your business. Please ensure you choose people who will spend adequate time with you and are dedicated to you and this role.

To bring them on board you will give them an official invitation and remember to add a term to it maybe a year or two so you can review for renewal if they served well, or tenure termination if they could not find time off their busy schedule to fulfil the role. Either way, you must send an appreciation letter to all members of your Board of Advisors.

Below is an example of an advisory board invitation letter.

**P.S.: Use Company's letterhead**

Dear Mrs...........................

### ADVISORY BOARD INVITATION LETTER.

I am pleased to invite you to join the Board of Advisors of (company name) for the year (duration). I am aware that your vast experience in business management, startups, alongside your network would be a tremendous asset to our success.

Operating since (month and year), (give brief introduction of your company and its products). (Say company's vision, mission, and goals.)

The principal purpose of our Business Advisory Board is to provide business development / growth advice around specified focus area. It is important that your involvement makes a tangible, measurable, and profitable contribution. It is also important that you are inspired to support (business name) over time, and to focus your energies on successfully and efficiently contributing to our company goals.

This Board will meet once a quarter (4 times in a year) (feel free to choose the frequency of meeting), and each meeting comprises a meal and two to four hours of focused discussions.

There may also be a need for some follow ups by email. Due to the matters to be discussed, members will need to sign a confidential agreement.

Thanks for reading and considering being a part of (company name).

While I look forward to your response, I am available to discuss any questions you may have.

Yours' faithfully,

Company Director's name.

For: (company's name)

## THE MANAGEMENT

The management runs the day-to-day affairs of the enterprise. This includes the executive directors and senior staff or head of departments. Some directors may not work in the business daily; they are called *non-executive directors*. Members of the management team comprise the top staff like Heads of Departments or unit directors. They are employees who work at the highest level of their department. They work hand-in-hand with the directors or business owners to create order and control in the workplace.

The boards and the management determine the strategic planning of the business, that is the long-term goals.

## Chapter Six

# HUMAN RESOURCES MANAGEMENT

*Human Resource Management* (HRM) is the process of managing people in organisations in a structured and thorough manner. The goal is to effectively use employees while reducing risks and maximising return on investment. It is the practice of recruiting, hiring, deploying, and managing an organisation's employees. Some refer to it as Human Resources (HR).

Business owners will have to attract talented workers to work for their organisations, as well as keep their loyalty. For start-ups, hiring skilled workers may be difficult as most start-ups do not have the financial capacity to do so, so they may have to hire average workers and through training and growing, make a skilled worker out of them.

## HUMAN RESOURCE MANAGEMENT

## A STAR

A-ATTRACTION
S- SELECTION
T- TRAINING
A- ASSESSMENT
R- REWARD

Created by: Yemisi Adeyeye
Author, Entrepreneurship is a beautiful thing         www.yemisiadeyeye.com

To build your workforce you will have to employ workers and the first step for that is attraction.

### ATTRACTION

Attraction of staff into an organisation is one of

the main HR activities and usually the first step towards acquiring skilled employees or talent to build competitive advantage (Holland, Sheehan & De Cieri 2007).

How do you get the attention of would-be staff?

How do you communicate to others that you need a particular type of worker?

First, you must know what position you want to fill and be able to answer the following questions correctly:

What job will the person do? What is the job prescription? What are the qualifications required for the post?

Are there any gender specifications?

Are there any other requirements by the company's leadership? Always balance your requirement with the employment laws of your country.

Your aim is to attract star employees into your company. First, you must think about where these kinds of people are and how to get their attention so they can apply for job.

Some companies may choose not to run advert, instead, they get recommendations from referees and work on it. We hired our first accountant in Lifefount Hospital through recommendation from another company who had no vacancy for accountant but got too many applications for the post.

What mode of communication will you use to attract potential staff? You can use traditional methods like printing in newspapers and magazines. You can print vacancy on fliers and post in your neighborhood or newspaper if you think it will work. You can attract potential employees through recruitment agencies, references from current employees, referrals, or recommendations from trusted people or other employees.

It is easier to use social media or internet to propagate vacancies and attract potential employees, since the coverage is wider; but remember to put deadlines on your advert so people will not keep sending applications after you've found the right fit. After getting all the interested CVs, the next thing is the interview stage and the selection phase.

## SELECTION

Selection is the process of interviewing and

picking the qualified person who can successfully do the tasks loaded in a job position while giving valuable contributions to the organisational growth. A selection system includes job analysis and following company policy while searching for the right fit without neglecting the certification, the soft skills, and core skills needed to fit the job position perfectly. This ensures that the selection criteria are job related and will provide meaningful organisational value.

Do you have documented process of hiring workers? If no, please document what your hiring process will be. By doing this, you are putting structures in your business. You can allow others to handle some duties on your behalf and they will do it as documented so you can have time for other managerial responsibilities.

What is your interview process like? What are the test modes? Are they oral, written, or computer based? What relevant questions will be asked? Who is in charge of the interview? Answer these questions and see how structured and organised the hiring processes will be.

Dear entrepreneur, do not hire someone whom you will need permission before firing. Refuse all influences so you can hire the right person in your organisation. It's okay to listen to suggestions but only hire someone that is fit for the role. Follow your company's policy and let everyone know your stand so that if you need to fire an employee, you will not need to take anyone's permission.

In this selection phase, you shortlist the CVs and pick those that will likely match the available positions, then you invite them for an interview which could be oral, written, or both. This can be done physically or virtually using various online video applications like Skype, WhatsApp, Zoom, etc.

After interviewing the candidates, the business owner or organisation will choose the best fit for the job. Criteria used for selection differs; it depends on what the occasion warrants, the position, and projects at hand. For most small to medium scale businesses, we value experience over education. Although for professional positions like that of a medical doctor in a hospital, the educational qualification is very important, and the experience is a great advantage.

When you select the eligible candidate, you must give him the following documents.

- Employment letter on company's letterheaded paper.

- Employees' data form, which the new staff will

sign along.

- Acceptance letter.

All these must be in duplicate. You will then:

- Open a file for the new staff.
- Give him a staff's identification number, and
- File copies of the letters in it.

Content of employment letter includes but is not limited to:

- Employee's biodata.
- Employee's designation or position.
- Employee's job description.
- Salary amount and all relevant or statutory deductions.
- Probation period and length of the period. This helps him to know when he becomes a permanent staff and when to expect a pay raise.
- Policy on disengagement.
- Notification of adherence to all company's

policies and guidelines.

This employment letter saved me from personnel issues when one of my employees, who was employed as an administrative officer, requested to be paid higher like the newly employed accountant, because he studied accounting too. He was quickly referred to his appointment letter, the designation, and job description and afterwards, told to do what he was employed and paid for, which quenched the fire immediately.

Many headaches business owners have with employees are due to the lack of documented processes. To have peace of mind and make your business grow, please document each step of your processes. If you don't have these documents and cannot hire a HR manager, develop one yourself, but if you can hire one, do so. You still have to communicate your idea on that process to the consultant or manager, which will form your company's culture.

## ONBOARDING OR TRAINING

The next thing to do is *onboarding*. When you are in an airplane, at the beginning of each flight, the pilot and the crew will welcome you on board and tell you the things you need to know about the airline, crew, pilots, safety measures, height at which the plane will cruise, where the convenience is located, etc. These are called the *onboarding information*. These, you will also do as you bring a new staff on board. You must develop a policy for onboarding.

You will brief the new employees on your company's structures, vision, mission, core values, slogan, organogram, and their job description. Also, train them on the standard operating procedure of each task they will perform. Afterwards, place them where they can learn from other employees doing similar work.

Training is one of the most essentials of human resource management. As it is said, 'if you do not train them, do not blame them'. Training and retraining of all employees are the key to obtaining peace of mind in your business. The business owner, HR manager or team, or external consultants can do the training.

At a time in Lifefount Hospital, we noticed our housekeeping department needed to improve; so, we got a consultant to train the team. This brought about a mind shift and an improvement we desired. In business accounting, training and research is an item, so put it in your budget and expend it to get peace of mind and business growth.

You must communicate the vision to everyone until everyone sees and seeks same focus. After creating policies and procedures, the management or the head of department must put internal control in place to ensure that everyone is in line with the company goals and also monitor the employees to ensure they do the things that are documented.

### Policies, Processes, And Standard Operating Procedure (SOP)

Policy is a course or principle of action adopted or proposed by an individual or organisation. Company's policies are the laws documented to guide and govern a company. They mould the company's culture.

Processes are series of events which produce results. You must document the events as they follow each other. Document process flows in different arms of your business. Consider your processes and ensure it is seamless and efficient.

Standard Operating Procedures are a set of specific human resource procedures based on laws, State Personnel Board Rules, regulations, guidelines, etc., to be followed in carrying out human resource processes.

It is the stepwise instructions on how to carry out

each task to achieve same great result, always. This makes clients and outsiders notice that you have a culture as each staff does the task excellently.

Lifefount's SOP on answering front-desk phone calls says that the front desk officer must pick the call and say, 'Thank you for calling Lifefount Hospital, (officer mentions his name) is on the line, how may I help you?' The phone, however, must not ring out more than once.

Your duty as a business owner is to ensure that your company's policies and processes are documented and you also ensure compliance.

This serves as a law guiding staff-to-staff, staff-to-client or staff-to-management interactions.

Please note that policies can be reviewed at designated intervals or as a need arises. You need to regularly and effectively communicate your policies to your staff so you can get a great buy-in from them.

Do a monthly or quarterly staff meeting to train your employees on different aspect of your business so each can understand his role in the scheme of running the business and can achieve organisational goals collectively.

As a small business owner, you will train both old and new staff by yourself or get a staff who understands your organisational goals to train others. You can also engage experts in related fields to train your staff. One of the consultants hired by Lifefount Hospital was in cleaning and waste management sector. He trained our staff on cleaning the hospital and it tremendously impacted how our housekeepers view their jobs as they were made to understand that they are very valuable. A clean environment is in the scheme of our healthcare delivery and they learnt ways to improve their cleaning processes.

Also, you will hand them the written documents containing the processes, SOPs, and policies so they can digest and acknowledge that they are informed and will obey all the instructions. Afterwards, keep a copy in the staff's file. This is a way to get your staff to buy into your vision and ideas and they, in turn, will help you to achieve them.

Do monthly meetings where you train and retrain your staff on your policies and culture. This strengthens internal processes, improve staff's understanding of your business and their performances. It's important to meet with your team or members of staff regularly so everyone is carried along in your moves towards organisational goals.

Also, document all communications including queries and staff responses. Always make your staff sign that they received original copies for all meetings, if you use paper for documentation. You must document your policies on all aspects of your processes. For example, resumption policy with sanction measures for defaulters, handing over policy, daily cash sales handling policy, annual leave policy, maternity leave policy, and casual leave policy. All policies should include sanctions for defaulters.

## STAFF'S PERFORMANCE ASSESSMENT OR APPRAISAL

An employee's performance appraisal is a process, often combining written and oral elements, whereby management evaluates and provides feedback on employee's job performance, including steps to improve or redirect activities as needed, an avenue by which they can be rewarded or recognised for a job done well which should not only be done in building a case to terminate an employee like in some organisations.

You must have ways of assessing each staff's soft skills and performance vis-à-vis his job description. You can do this assessment monthly or quarterly as the organisation deems fit or as documented in its policy.

Performance appraisal is supposed to be a *developmental experience* for the employee and a *teaching moment* for the manager, not a *dreaded moment* which forfeits its purpose.

Employer should try to establish the performance appraisal process as a dialogue in which the ultimate purpose is the betterment of all parties.

Performance appraisal and development helps to achieve these for your business:

- Improve the company's productivity.

- Make informed personnel decisions regarding promotion, job changes, and termination.

- Identify the goals and responsibilities of a job.

- Assess an employee's performance against these goals.

- Work to improve the employee's performance by naming specific areas for improvement, develop a plan aimed at improving these areas, support the employee's efforts at improvement via feedback and assistance, and ensure the employee's involvement and commitment to improving his performance.

### Factors to Consider to Know the Type of Appraisal to Do

The size of employees determines what mode an appraisal will undergo. Oral or traditional appraisal may be impossible for companies with large staff sizes and those with employees on an alternative work schedule, like work-from-home employees. It is better to make it into a written format.

Self-appraisal may be biased, therefore, a *360-degrees feedback*, which employees, manager's assessment, review of other employees the staff interacts with (peer evaluation), external (customers) and management performance (upward appraisals) can provide, is very important.

As a company grows in size, a small business owner should consider using 360-degree feedback to appraise employees. Communication in a business of ten people varies wildly from that of a company of 100 persons, and 360-degree feedback ensures that an employee's performance is observed by those who work most closely with him.

Small business owners or managers can either include the feedback in the performance review or choose to provide it informally for developmental purposes.

The results of a performance appraisal are often used to support a promotion, termination, salary increase, or job/position change; they are looked at closely in employee's discrimination suits.

## REWARDS AND REMUNERATION

This leads to staff's motivation and retention. It may be hard to believe, but recognition is the most powerful motivator of all. (Hansen et al., 2002). Here are things to do to reward your employees:

- Recognise and openly appreciate consistent good work.
- Give bonuses.
- Give promotions.
- Give benefits (healthcare package, cooperative loans, etc.) and awards.
- Give a letter of commendation for outstanding performances.

One of the challenges of business owners, especially small businesses, is high employees' turnover, which results from employees leaving small companies after working for a short time due to different reasons. Employers are therefore saddled with the responsibility of hiring new employees to replace the ones who left. There are things to do to reduce employees' turnover and retain quality employees for a very long time. In Lifefount Hospital, we have those that have been with us almost throughout our business existence. They are very productive, responsible, and dependable.

What makes it easier for employees to remain in an organisation for a long time includes the job satisfaction they get from working with your organisation. One of the few things that improve job satisfaction includes employees' abilities to improve their personal development and the structures they see in your organisation.

As a business owner, your duty is to document or get others to document your processes to make working with you attractive. As you know, words get to potential staff about how structured your organisation is.

We get a lot of unsolicited job applications from interested applicants and I believe they must have heard or perceived our business' structure and culture. Your managers' leadership characteristics and yours are also very important in improving your employees' retention. Pay may attract the right employees, but these factors will keep them working for you for a long time.

Lead your staff with empathy but also be firm and adhere to your policies so fairness is seen in your dealings. That way, you will earn their respect and not force it out of them.

Great working environment, mutual respect, appropriate tools, equipment and protection, fairness, consistency in dispensing hope through organisational vision, communication and assurance of staff's future, etc.

helps in reducing turnover in your company. Act like you care genuinely, and reward excellent contribution.

Remember, your staff is your number one customer; they are also called *internal customer* and when you treat them right, they will treat your customers and business right, leading to productivity, profitability, and business growth.

## Chapter Seven

# MARKETING: THE SEVEN STEPS TO MAKING HUGE SALES AND GAINING BRAND LOYALTY

Marketing is an important aspect of business which every business owner and company must master. In fact, as the owner of a small business, you are the Chief Marketing Officer (CMO) of your enterprise.

Marketing has 3 basic aims:

- To introduce product, service, or company to an audience.

- To convert audiences to buyers, or to bring sales.

- To make buyers returning customers and increase brand loyalty.

The ability to get your offer to the ideal customer is essential to your business's success.

'Marketing is a way to connect the products and services you offer with customers who want and need such products and services. It is multi-faceted, starting with researching your target market and how best to deliver the message to coming up with a plan to execute your promotion via various marketing media. The goal is to develop a strategy to create, price and distribute your products and services for an exchange that will satisfy both you and your customers' objectives. It is an ever-evolving process—always evaluating that your message still meets the needs and wants of your market'. – Trish Green (Executive Vice President, Head of Marketing, Student Funding Group, LLC).

Before you market, you must know what you want to achieve at the end. As much as you want to satisfy your customer's needs in your marketing approach, don't forget you must meet your company's goals of profitable sales, too. Let us look at some key aspects of marketing that are relevant as you make strategic marketing plans, which usually include marketing research and others:

1. **Marketing Strategy**

    Marketing strategy refers to a business's overall game plan for reaching prospective consumers and turning them into customers of the products or services.

2. **Market Research**

    Market research is the process of evaluating the possibility of making sales from a new product or service of your company by conducting research in which you seek information from or about potential consumers.

    Before selling your products and services, do a survey or administer a questionnaire asking questions that will make you know your potential customer's feelings about what you are about to embark on.

    A small business can do the survey directly or engage a marketing agency to present a sample or a survey and get potential customers' opinions.

Analyse the details gathered from the market—their responses, reactions, and opinions, to have an overview of the range of those your company will concentrate on (target market) or see if there is a need to modify your product or service in order to get more people interested in your offering.

**3. Marketing Plan**

A marketing plan is a section of your business plan which outlines your marketing strategy and tactics. It's usually focused on a specific period (i.e., over the next 12 months).

**4. Marketing Budget**

While making your marketing strategy, create a marketing budget alongside. Many business owners, especially small businesses, don't give a budget to marketing. They either do not engage in marketing or practice little marketing.

A marketing budget outlines all the money a business intends to spend on marketing-related projects for the year or quarter of the year. Marketing budgets can include expenses such as paid advertisement, sponsored web content, new marketing staff, a registered blog domain and marketing automation software, and social media paid ads.

Marketing can be expensive so you don't want to spend your budget on activities that will not convert to sales and thus, bringing the company a huge loss. It is therefore very important that you must know who your target customer and target market is, and how to reach them with the right message, at the right time, while getting the right response.

## 5. Target Market

A target market refers to a group of consumers or customers to whom a company wants to sell its products and services to, and to whom it directs its marketing efforts. Consumers who make up a target market share similar characteristics including geography, buying power, demographics, and incomes.

Target marketing involves aiming your marketing efforts at specific group of consumers. This will make the promotion, pricing, and distribution of your products or services easier and more cost effective. It provides a focus to all of your marketing activities. Therefore, resist the temptation of trying to serve everyone in the hopes of getting a larger slice of the market.

## 6. Market Segmentation

This is the process of dividing a target market into smaller, more-defined categories. It segments customers and audiences into groups that share similar characteristics such as demographics, interests, needs, or location.

The four bases of market segmentation are:

- **Demographic Market Segmentation**

    This is especially good for businesses that sell directly to customers (B2C). Examples in this category include age, gender, income, location, family situation, annual income, education, and ethnicity. For businesses that sell directly to other businesses (B2B), demographic market segmentation that will be considered includes company size, industry, and job function.

- **Psychographic Market Segmentation**

    Examples include personality traits, values, attitudes, interests, lifestyles, psychological influences, subconscious and conscious beliefs, motivations, and priorities. These examples help you tailor your marketing to suit your customer's personality and psychology perfectly.

- **Behavioural Market Segmentation**

    Behavioural market segmentation examples include purchasing habits, spending habits, user status, and brand interactions.

- **Geographic Market Segmentation**

    Examples include: ZIP code, city, state, country, radius around a certain location, climate, and urban or rural area. There are several geographic parameters you can use to segment your target market. These are:

a) Location: Segmenting your target market by location can be by cities, towns, or different continents. This can be used to estimate or identify a new geographic location you may wish to expand your business to.

b) Climate: Market segmentation by climate helps you clarify and know where the climatic conditions are more appropriate for your products or services.

c) **Culture:** This is one of the geographic parameters which helps you segment your target market based on cultural diversities. Before dividing your target market into more-defined categories, you need to check for the cultural diversities of such market. Check for their symbols and representations as this will help you know how best to provide value and stay relevant in the market. For example, in Western cultures, white symbolises purity, peace, cleanliness, and elegance but in some instances, it is a different representation in China. In China, it symbolises death, bad luck, and mourning as it is commonly worn at funerals.

d) **Population:** Segmenting by population involves you considering the density or population type of several areas before setting up your business there. Will your products serve a densely-populated area well or a less-populated area? Will it thrive in an over-populated or under-populated area? Check for what population or areas your products and services can serve better before setting up your business as this will determine how well your ideal market will respond to your offer. You can also overlay demographic information here to find target audiences.

e) Language: This calls for a proper understanding of your target market. You must speak your audiences' languages before your business can thrive. You cannot market a product to a Chinese market while speaking Spanish. You need to speak the main language that suits your audiences so that they can understand you and the offer you are selling to them.

f) Urban, suburban, and rural: When segmenting your market, you need to identify these three environments and the marketing strategies to use for them. Those in urban and suburbs tend to have more purchasing power than those in rural areas, therefore, products can be more expensive than the other with respect to locations.

## Benefits of Market Segmentation

(a) When you know who you're talking to, you will be able to create stronger marketing messages and target it at them. This is more effective than using general and vague languages while speaking to non-specific and general audiences.

(b) You will be able to know the most effective marketing tactics that fit the audience you are targeting, the best solutions to their problems, and the great methods for reaching them.

(c) You will be able to design hyper-targeted ads. When you use market segmentation to define your audiences using their peculiar characteristics, you will be able to create more effective and targeted digital ad campaigns.

(d) You will attract quality leads and convert them to sales. You draw in ideal prospects and are more likely to turn your potential customers into buyers.

(e) You will be able to differentiate your brand from your competitor's. When you are more specific about your value propositions and how you communicate them, this will also make you unique from competitors.

(f) You will develop stronger customer attraction for your brand.

(g) You will be able to identify and take advantage of niche market opportunities. The more focused you are, the more opportunities to serve a market segment you will see.

(h) It keeps your message focused by keeping your messages and marketing objectives on track.

## 7. Customer Avatar

Create an avatar with an understanding of your target market. Customer avatar is a mental image of what your ideal customers are like; it helps you to get into your customers' minds. In creating an avatar, you temporarily become your ideal customer.

An avatar is a detailed exploration and description of your target customers and their lives. It helps you tell their story so that you can visualise life from their perspectives, not yours.

Avatars get you right into the mind of your prospects, which is very crucial when crafting your message to your target market.

## 8. Marketing Mix

Marketing mix is the set of marketing tools that most firms used to pursue their marketing objectives in the target market. Thus, marketing mix refers to *four* broad levels of marketing decisions: product, price, place, and promotion. Three additional ones which are also relevant to service businesses are people, process, and physical environment. All these make up the *Marketing Mix*. These are key ingredients that will ensure growth and success of your business.

Deep understanding of the marketing mix saves a business from dying. What good is it when you have a fantastic product or service and no one neither knows about it, nor buys it?

## 1. Marketing Mix: Product

To get customers for your product, you must produce with the user in mind.

You might need to ask these questions which will help

you produce items fit for your customer's needs and wants:

- What is the product's name?
- Is the product's name attractive and unoffensive?
- Is the product needed by clients?
- How and where will the client use it?
- What does the client want from the service or product?
- How is the product or service different from others?
- What are the features clients desire?
- What are the sizes or colours available?

## 2. Marketing Mix: Price

This is very important, most especially, for general goods. The price of the product is basically the amount a customer pays to enjoy it. Price is a very important component of the marketing mix definition. You get it right, you stay; but if you get it wrong, it may affect sales. New businesses may have the challenge of getting customers to pay a high price as they are not well known. To arrive at a profitable price, you must answer these questions:

- How much did it cost you to make the product?
- What are the customers' perceived product value?
- Do you think that the slight price decrease could significantly increase your market share?

- Can the current price of the product keep up with that of your competitors' products?

Do not forget to consider competitor's prices, here.

There are three major pricing strategies, and these are:

### a) Market penetration pricing

Wikipedia describes market penetration pricing as a pricing strategy where the price of a product is initially set low to reach a wide fraction of the market rapidly and initiate words of mouth. The strategy works on the expectation that customers will switch to the new brand because of the lower price.

### b) Market skimming pricing

According to PM Group, it is 'a method of pricing involving setting a high initial price for a high-end product to attract buyers with suitable resources who also have a strong want for the product'. The purpose of market skimming is to secure as much revenue from the product before competing, low-end products appear. When this happens, the seller usually lowers the price of their high-end product considerably to corner the low-end of the market as well. This pricing strategy is common in the technological industry.

c) **Neutral pricing**

In a neutral pricing, the prices are set by the general market, with your prices just at your competitors' prices. The major benefit of a neutral pricing strategy is that it works in all four periods in the life cycle. The major drawback is that your company is not maximising its profits by placing prices based only on the market. Essentially, neutral pricing is the safe way to play the pricing game, as described by Meissner Research Group.

3. **Marketing Mix: Place**

Placement or distribution is a very important part of the product mix definition. You have to position and distribute the product in a place that is accessible to potential buyers.

Where do your clients look for your service or product?

What kind of stores do potential clients go to?

Do they shop in a mall, open market, in the supermarket, or online?

How do you access the different distribution channels?

How is your distribution strategy different from your competitors?

Do you need a strong sales force? Do you need to attend trade fairs?

Do you need to sell in an online store?

Wherever your clients are, you need to get your product there. That's marketing!

## 4. Marketing Mix: Promotion

Promotion is a very important component of marketing as it can boost brand's recognition and sales. It comprises various elements, such as special offers, endorsements, user trials, direct mailing, educational fliers, leaflets, posters, gifts, competitions, collaborations, sales organisation, public relations, advertisement, and sales promotion.

In contemporary times, there seems to be a shift in focus from offline to the online world, and the appearance of the 2020 pandemic drove most businesses online. Public relations are communications that are typically not paid for, like words of mouth/client's testimonials. These are powerful marketing tools you can post on social media and your websites.

To get the best out of your promotion mix, you need to ask and answer this question:

How can you send marketing messages to your potential buyers?

When preparing your message, it is good to think through how you can summarise your business's offering in one minute such that an amateur will understand in a simple way. This is called *pitch deck* or *elevator pitch*.

As a business owner, being able to succinctly convey the problems you solve is a real art, especially if you're in a complex business. The idea is to grab your listeners' attention and make them understand in a way that they will patronise you immediately and recommend you to others.

Your elevator pitch must contain your product or service and its unique selling point. Knowing that you have 60 seconds to 90 seconds to deliver an audible and convincing speech, you must be concise and have a well-researched fact for your business and its value proposition. In whatever way you take your prospect through, it must be a journey that covers the problem, the solution, and the proof.

When is the best time to promote your product?

This question depends on the location or the platform where the promotion will take place. For example,

Instagram insights can give you an idea of the time when your page has higher traffic. If you are using the radio, you can target peak periods and place your adverts.

Which channel of promotion will make you reach your potential audience and buyers quickly?

Channel of promotion can be in person (in a physical environment) or through traditional and digital media.

Promotions held in physical environments allow for person-to-person interaction, which gives room for immediate purchases due to incentives like discounts, free items, games, and contests. Physical environments are special events such as concerts, festivals, trade shows, exhibitions, sports field, shopping malls or department stores with the use of ambassadors, promotional models, sales agents, or celebrities. Traditional media include print, electronic, and outdoor media.

- **Print Media**

  This involves using media, such as newspapers and magazines for promotions.

- **Electronic Media**

  Electronic media include using radio and television.

Many people listen to radio or watch television. Radio advert is cost effective compared to television advert. Electronic media can take your message directly into the hearts of the viewers or audiences who may likely become your customers. These media increase brand awareness, customer's pride in your brand, and loyalty to the same brand.

Going on air is one great way to market your product or service and get the message across to large audience, especially when using radio or TV stations, which your target market are loyal to.

- **Outdoor Media**

    This includes media such as banner or billboard advertisements. Each platform provides ways for brands to reach consumers via advertisements. Bill boards are popular tools in advertising and marketing products and services. Large companies spend huge amount of money annually on placing their products or services on boards where they are visibly displayed in densely-populated areas. Outdoor media create products or services awareness and they are constantly in the face of the passers-by.

    Traditional media still have their advantages as they help in ensuring brand visibility in a geographical territory. They also do better at reaching older people.

- **Digital Media**

You must decide on which digital media platform you will use in promoting your product.

Digital media is currently the most effective way for brands to reach their consumers daily. Over 2.7 billion people are online globally, which is about 40% of the world's population. 67% of all internet users globally use social media.

Social media, as a modern marketing tool, offer opportunities to reach larger audiences interactively. These interactions allow for conversation rather than simply educating the customer. Facebook, Snapchat, Instagram, Twitter, Pinterest, Tumblr, TikTok and alternate audio and media sites like Soundcloud and Mixcloud allow users to interact and promote music online at little or no cost.

You can purchase and buy ad space as well as get potential customer's interactions such as likes, followers, and clicks to your page with the use of third parties. As a participatory media culture, social media platforms or social networking sites are forms of mass communication that allow large amounts of product and distribution of content to reach the largest audience possible through media technologies, as described by Wikipedia.

Paid ads get you more promotion for your goods and services, but a business owner must understand the dynamics of paid ads or use an ad agency in order to get the best.

With paid ads, you can reach customers at an exact moment in time as customers search for related item or service.

There is no short cut to it; business owners must learn how to use social media to their advantage. COVID-19 pandemic hit most of the world in 2020 and there was a total lockdown in which movement of people and goods were stopped. When this happened, most people moved online. Digital media took centre stage and were used in promoting goods and services.

Mass communication has led to modern marketing strategies to continue focusing on brand awareness, large distributions, and heavy promotions. Social media took interaction with potential customers to a deeper level. The goal of a promotion is to reach the multitude in a time-efficient and a cost-effective manner.

Email marketing is the highly effective digital marketing strategy for sending emails to prospects and customers. Effective email marketing converts prospects into customers, and turns onetime buyers into loyal, raving fans.

Apps that make email marketing easier and effective are mailchimp, getresponse, convertkit, Aweber, Drip, Zoho campaigns, etc.

To use email marketing, you need to have an email list of those who are in your target market. To get emails of people interested in your product or service, you will need to give information or offers like eBooks, cheat sheet of tips or resources, white papers or case studies, webinar, free trials or sample, free quote or consultation, quizzes or a self-assessment, coupon, and any valuable content. These are called *lead magnets*.

Building a community online like creating a Facebook group, page, email list, or WhatsApp group can help with promoting your goods and services and gain brand loyalty.

What strategy of your competitors will you adopt or improve on?

5. **Marketing Mix: People**

   This consists of both target market and people directly related to the business. Thorough research is important to discover whether there are enough people in your target market who demand certain types of products and services.

   The company's employees are important in marketing because they are the ones who deliver the services.

   It is important to hire and train the right people to deliver superior service to the clients, whether they run a support desk, are customer service, copywriters, programmers, etc. Have human resource policy manual which are laws that guide activities and management of your staff. I developed a template that you can customise to fit your company's needs and culture, I would love to share with you provided you send me your request.

6. **Marketing Mix: Process**

   Your processes must be user friendly and effective so it can minimise cost. It could be your entire sales funnel, a pay system, distribution system, and other systematic procedures and steps to ensure an effective business.

   With how fabulous your marketing is and the leads it generates, if at the point of contact with your company the potential customers encountered any discomfort, you may lose them. So, think through your processes to ensure every step is user friendly. Don't forget that your goal is to get sales, therefore, make it easy for customers to buy.

### 7. Marketing Mix: Physical Evidence

In the service industries, there should be physical evidence that you delivered the service. Physical evidence also pertains to how a business and its products are perceived in the marketplace. It is the evidence of a business's presence and establishment.

There are market leaders or business owners who have established a physical evidence, as well as psychological evidence in their marketing.

They have manipulated their consumer perception so well to the point where their brands appear first in line when an individual is asked to broadly name a brand in their niche or industry.

With the right marketing mix and foundations in place, you are on your journey to becoming a successful brand. If your products or services are fantastic but customers don't know about them, they cannot buy them. Therefore, do all you can and get the right word out there.

Dear small business owner, know that you are the Chief Marketing Officer (CMO) for your business and always remember to *market, market,* and *market* your business. I will summarise this using the 4Cs of marketing by Robert F. Lauterborn in 1990, who created an extension (it's more like a summary to me) to the 4Ps of marketing mix.

- Cost: Cost is not the only cost incurred when purchasing a product, but also other costs involved until customers take ownership of the product.

- Consumers' wants and needs: A company should only sell a product that addresses consumers' demands. So, marketers and business researchers should carefully study the consumer's wants and needs.

- Communication: According to Lauterborn, 'promotion is *manipulative* while communication is *cooperative'*. Marketers should aim to create an open dialogue with potential clients based on their needs and wants.

- Convenience: The products should be readily available to the consumers. Marketers should strategically place the products at several visible distribution points.

## General Advantages of Marketing Your Business

- It gives your products and services brand visibility.
- It increases sales and improves business profits.
- It leads to new product ideas (from customers' opinion).
- It helps gain prospects.
- It helps a brand to gain customers' trusts.
- It builds credibility.
- It creates business expansion.
- It provides more revenue.
- It keeps a brand longer in the market space.

## General Disadvantages of Marketing

- Marketing is costly.
- It takes time.

## Disadvantages of Poor Marketing

- It makes you lose to competitors.
- It leads to wastage of resources.
- It also leads to little or no survival in the market space.
- It makes you unable to sustain your brand.
- It brings little or no sale.

At the end of your marketing processes, you want to go beyond people knowing your brand to turning your prospects to customers. The greatest reward of all is turning one-time customer to continuous and loyal customers who keep buying over and over again and one that keeps positive recommendations and testimonials about your business. To achieve sales, you need to pay close attention to the message you pass across and shoot in a way to achieve sales.

### Copywriting for Sales

Almost no other skill will reward you richly than the ability to write compelling words. Being able to articulate your words clearly tells why a prospect should buy from you rather than your competitors. Your words should create an emotion and motivate them to action. This is the master skill of marketing. Using monotone and boring sales copy is the fastest way of losing your customers' and prospects' interests.

### Target the Pain

Imagine you have a splitting headache; you open your medicine cabinet, start searching through your pack of half-used tablets, creams, and vitamins only to realise you are totally out of pain relief medication.

Immediately, you rushed down to your local pharmacy hoping to get the tablets that's going to give you relief you so desperately need. Do you worry about price? No?

Well, the usual way of shopping gets thrown out the window when we are in pain. The exact way is the same for your customer and prospect. So many times, businesses talk about *features* and *benefits* rather than speaking to the pain customers have. How many sales does a pharmacist need to get to sell pain-relief medication to someone with a splitting headache? Very little, I suspect.

### Create an Irresistible Offer

Now that you know what your market wants, you need to package it and present it as an irresistible offer. Here are some of the essential elements:

**Value:** What is the most valuable thing you could do for your customer?

**Language:** Learn the language used within your target market.

**Reason:** When you have a great offer, you need to justify why you're doing this.

**Value stacking:** Packing in many bonuses can make your offer be an easy decision to buy.

**Upsells:** When your prospect is hot and in the buying frame of mind, this is the perfect time to offer them a complimentary product or service.

**Payment plan:** This is absolutely critical for high-ticket items and can mean the difference between the customer balking and walking away or making the sale.

**Guarantee:** You need an outrageous guarantee because people have been disappointed so many times.

**Scarcity:** Your offer needs to have an element of scarcity—reason to make people respond immediately.

### Crafting Your Offer

Some supplementary questions that can help you craft your offer include:

- What is my target market really buying? (e.g., people don't really buy insurance; they buy peace of mind.)
- What is the biggest benefit to lead with?

- What are the best emotionally charged words and phrases that will capture and hold the attention of this market?
- What objectives do my prospects have and how will I solve them?
- What outrageous offer (including a guarantee) can we make?
- Is there an intriguing story we can tell?
- Who else is selling something similar to my product or service, and how?
- Who else has tried selling them something similar, and how has that effort failed?

One of the reasons marketing campaigns fail is because the offer is lazy and poorly thought out.

### Category of Power Words

1. Words that highlight urgency like running out, last chance, fast selling out, hurry now, limited offer, and deadline.

2. Words that give assurance like money-back guarantee, lifetime offer, no risk, endorsed, verified, and protected.

3. Words that play on pain points like pain, mistakes, failure, risk, loss, stress, pitfalls, and hate.

4. Words that show exclusivity and/or curiosity: you are the first to hear it, private, limited seats, members only, subscribers only, be one of the few, insiders only, etc.

These words play on the customer's emotions, as every decision to buy is emotional.

### Different Emotions of Customers

Sales or selling is an emotional thing and you can use some words that stimulate different emotions in prospects that may take all the important steps of buying your product or service. There are several emotions customers display:

- **Prudence**

    When you talk about the money they will save by buying your product, it will appeal to a prudent mind. This mind thinks of the statement: if I decide now, I will be rewarded.

    Your copywriting can create the fear emotion, especially when you tell stories of those who did not act and what happened to them. Your prospects who are afraid of such consequences will take the step to buy.

- **Envy**

    Another emotion used to get buying customer is envy. When you make comments like we have worked with leading or foremost brands like (mentioning their competitors), envy will make them buy from you so they can be on par with their competitors.

- **Altruism**

    Altruism is another emotion you can leverage during marketing to get prospects to buy, by making them see the good works they did when they buy your product. For example, buying this product will assist us in sending one of our farmer's children to elementary school. Such buyers connect buying with good deeds and then buy more.

- **Pride**

    When you sell with words that show that important people use the product or service, it gives a sense of pride, value, and respect. When you display awards or trophies won because of the class of your product or service, it depicts excellence and status.

- **Shame**

    When your words point to the client's previous mistakes and how your products can prevent them, such client will want to seal the deal to avoid future error and shame and buy from you immediately.

'No customer, No Business'.

– *Yemisi Adeyeye*

## Chapter Eight

# CUSTOMER RELATIONSHIP MANAGEMENT

A customer, they say, is king. Once there is no customer, there is no business. Therefore, the sole aim of a business is to retain customers.

A customer is an individual or company who purchases goods, services, products, or an idea from a seller or another company. As a business owner, you must know who your ideal customers are, as this will help you plan the best way to satisfy them. When your customers are satisfied, they will not only pay you but also be loyal to your brand.

Sometimes, aside from paying for purchases, satisfied customers also show gratitude for the value added to them. How gratifying it is for a business owner to get paid and also receive an appreciation from a satisfied customer. Understanding your target customers will help you define and refine your products to suit your customers' needs and wants. Understanding your customers will move you to fine-tune your process so that their user experiences are smooth.

Your processes must be easy for customers to navigate. It must be easy to pay and receive what they paid for. User experience must also be without hassles by removing complexities from accessing you or your product.

Dear business owner, you must know some details about your target customer like their characteristics, habits, demands for your service or product, sentiments, spending trends, and preferences.

When you are clear on who your ideal customers are and how to serve them uniquely, you will give a value that differentiates you from others and keeps them coming back for more. You can classify your customers according to the level and type of interaction you have with the.

## TYPES OF CUSTOMERS.

### 1) Potential Customers

A potential customer is a customer at the beginning of interaction with your business. They are the ones who ask questions and sometimes the *I will get back to you* kinds. They are also customers who get their appetites stimulated after a nice sponsored advert but need nurturing and warming up before deciding.

They are interested in your business either by filling a contact form, signing up for your weekly newsletters, or asking a question through direct message (DM).

The interest separates them from others. Use that spark of interest to convert them into paying customers. You need to follow the lead diligently to convert them to paying customers. To do this, you must do two things: show them value and let them know you are always available for more interaction and communication.

You must show potential customers the value they will get from your product by demonstrating it or point them to a resource that will convince them to buy, e.g., a landing page or document that will convert them.

If they are not buying immediately, let them know they can always ask for help or advice from you. They will be glad about your offer.

## 2) New Customers

They are fresh customers who just bought something from you. A new customer is learning how to use your product; therefore, you must support them through their adoption period.

I once bought a fantastic accounting software with no after sale service. Navigating the software was tedious and stressful and the subscription ended without me getting the proposed value. I bought again, paying about four times more to access some forms of support, but I couldn't get the support I needed. At the end, I stopped buying the expensive software despite my interest in the product and the ability to pay. I hope with this, you understand why investing time to guide a new customer is very vital.

However, let them have a contact option for future communication.

## 3) Impulsive Customers

These ones can change their mind anytime regarding their purchases. They make a buying decision instantly, provided they have the right conditions. They also do not need much persuasion or warm up with value proposition.

Just make buying process easy for them so they can buy instantly. When your process is long or complex, you lose them. Make checking out easy, provide concise help or quick support, and see how you will get them buying instantly.

## 4) Discount Customers

This customer sees value in your product but will not buy it at full price. They always want a discount and will appreciate it no matter how small it is. If you are offering a service at a discounted price, such customers stop buying immediately the discount stops.

To increase your chances of keeping a discount customer, you need to show them that they will not only get a product at a discount, but will get amazing customer service bundled with their purchase.

You need to provide added value that will make discount customers think twice and stick with you and not switch to another company.

**5) Loyal Customers**

No matter your price, they stay loyal; they never leave. They also keep coming back for more. They have a significant impact on your revenue and they become your brand's ambassadors.

Your business grows by their words of mouth referrals. They recommend your business or product to their friends and family and are instrumental to you, as you have a healthy stream of new customers always.

You want to leverage on their experiences and understand what makes them so satisfied with your business?

Ask for the aspects of your products or business they like the most, take note of them, and make sure they are always available for them and new customers to enjoy.

Give your loyal customers a platform like a client's testimonial slot on your website, feature one of them in a case study, or use as social proof on your landing pages. This will appeal to potential customers.

### 6) Daring Customers

These customers comprise the rude, nasty, troublemakers, and those who love undue attention. Treat them as an unhappy customer but make sure your company's offering is delivered and do not be rude to them. Instead, let them see you are on their side or you let the calmest person in your team handle them.

### 7) Unhappy Customers

Your unhappy customers give you the best opportunity to learn how to become better.

Identify their complaint and proffer possible solutions while communicating what you are doing or hope to do to make them happy.

Listen and apologise to them, and call them. When they know their concerns have been escalated to the top without them asking for it, many will be pleased and know their opinions count.

You also need to monitor your customer service channels and social media for any issues you need to fix and fix them immediately.

After apologising, you can offer them a

small compensation to gain their loyalty. This works better than doing nothing and eventually losing customers.

## TYPES OF CUSTOMER RELATIONSHIP

The essence of customer relationship structure is to manage clients/customers. The system allows business owners to put the customers first by providing, collecting, and applying information about them to come up with better value proposition for the customers.

There are basically four types of customer relationship that managements employ. They are: analytical, collaborative, operative, and communicative customer relationships.

### 1) Analytical Customer Relationship

Data collected from customers can be analysed through several means. However, the analytical customer relationship system analyses collected data electronically. These customers' data could include contact, customers' properties, and information derived from both online and offline behaviour. The detail can be used to determine responses, and it involves all operations that do not directly deal with customers.

### Benefits:

- Creation of customers' database.
- Creation of sales history.
- Access to customers' feedbacks.
- Saves time since customers/clients are not directly involved.
- Enable business owners to consider customers in their organisational plans.

## 2) Collaborative Customer Relationship

An organisation or business comprises various departments of a company, such as sales, technical support, and marketing, which share any information they collect from the interactions with customers. This is used as customers' feedbacks to benefit the business.

As the name implies, it is the ability of these various departments to treat the data collected and devise strategies that allow them to offer optimum service and strengthen interaction.

## Benefits:

1. Flexibility: it is easy to manage changes since the activity cuts across different departments with different ranges of expertise.
2. Innovation: it provides more creative ideas to work on.
3. It helps facilitate strategic thinking.
4. It also brings forth emerging clients.
5. Promotion of improved capacity.
6. It ensures geographical spread.

## 3) Operative Customer Relationship (OCR)

According to e-commerce Wikipedia, Operative Customer Relationship (OCR) is the task of an operative manager to manage a company's customers' contacts to gain customer's information and this can comprise existing and future contacts with a support function for all departments having customers' contacts.

### The 3 main components of OCR are:

- Marketing automation
- Sales automation, and
- Service automation.

**Marketing Automation:** The process makes it easier to create a target population and measure the efficiency of allocated resources. All marketing processes are integrated and directly linked to the customer.

**Sales Automation:** Sale automation is used to improve the efficiency of tasks like inventory controls, sales processing, contact managing, scheduling, and tracking of customer interactions, as well as analysing sales forecast and performance.

**Service Automation:** Service automation is used predominantly for service functions such as administrative support (contacts, products availability, and delivery time). This is based on customers-initiated contact, such as offerings and complaint management.

### 4) Communicative Customer Relationship

There is a need to cover all communications with the customers, such as individual customer interaction through a direct interface with the client by which all the planning and the actual communication with the customer take place. It also includes measures to control and support the communication channels towards the customer.

### Benefits:

1. Customers can relate directly with company.
2. There is little or no complexity in interaction procedures.
3. Customers get to relay complaints directly to the company.
4. It ensures customers' satisfaction.
5. More flexible than other forms of customer relationships.

### The Mastery of Customer Relationship

Like every other kinds of relationship, customer relationship is essential to build trust, retain patronage, and ultimately drive sales. For your business to succeed, you must master the skill of having a good relationship with customers.

Be knowledgeable about your customers' characteristics; the more you know about them, the more you can help them.

Always make your customers feel great by being a proactive problem solver.

The function of a good customer relationship management is to establish, develop, and maintain a good relationship with customers while giving them a sense of relevance.

Customers want to know if you care about them or you are only interested in the selling and buying relationship. Think of it; you would like to feel good after spending your money, so do your buyers also want to feel good. Some customers feel connected to your brand like they are an extension of your business family, but what should you do to family? You should care about them and show them they are very important to you. Sometimes, you tell your family that they are your priority. This is same for business family members; they want to feel like they are your priority too.

As a business owner, it may not be physically possible to be all things to all customers. That is why you need a customer service department saddled with these post-purchase engagements. Let all your employees know that irrespective of their department or unit, everyone is part of customer service delivery team. You want each step of customers' interaction with your company to be superb, thus creating a lasting and beautiful impression.

Every customer has the potential to grow; so, treat both notable and occasional customers with respect and dignity. The more your customers grow, the more they do business with you and the more your business grows.

Customer relationship is key in business success and there are ways to ensure all customers, both current and potential, are well documented and followed up. Here are five ways to set up a customer relationship plan:

1. Collect and document details of customers at the very first time you do business with them.
2. Create a mailing list, broadcast list, or other forms of messaging channels.
3. Determine when to send complimentary messages, e.g., birthday, New Year, or national festive periods.
4. Send checkup messages and encourage customers to give you feedback.
5. Tell them you would love to know whichever way you can be of help.

One way to get customers in and make them feel you care about them is to always make them perceive you are helping them solve a problem, which you actually should be doing.

## Advantages of A Good Customer Relationship Management

There are several advantages of mastering

customer relationship, and they are:

1. Customers feel important and are willing to keep patronising you.
2. Customers trust you and give less attention to your competitors.
3. It makes you know your customers better.
4. It helps you get a referral from customers who feel you care about them.
5. It also helps you track business history.
6. It helps drive sales with retention of customers.
7. It strengthens your brand.

## Methods of Mastering Customer Relationship.

- **Communication**

    Communication is the fuel of any relationship. Whether you provide a service or sell a product, your ability to keep communicating with customers will fetch you more support. By developing a good communication structure that allows customers to hear from you often and vice versa, you've created a great channel of communication. This communication is easier with social media, where users can give you feedback and get more information that will help them adopt your product.

- **Listening**

    As much as you are the one selling to them and you stand the position to talk more, creating time to listen to what your customers have to say is one way to build good customer relationship. Customers will often have complaints due to individual differences, preference, and business background. If such complaints aren't well managed, it could lead to a gap between you and them. Listening is an art all business owners and their team must learn.

    What every customer wants is a service provider who listens to their challenges and attempt to provide solutions without looking down on them. More importantly, don't leave any part of your customer's complaints untouched. You must receive and attend to them very well. The moment customers realise your willingness to listen and provide solutions to their concerns, they will respect and keep you strongly in mind. Kindly note that your willingness to help your customers determines the level at which you keep them glued to your brand.

- **Satisfaction**

    People believe that it is difficult to satisfy

customers. That idea, however, is relative. With a good structure, entrepreneurs can provide services that satisfy the largest portion of their customers. Customers too can sense how much you have invested into what you have to offer. They can sense when a product is quality or not and when your service is shallow or excellent.

Make your efforts obvious. For example, you can let them in on how much time goes into the production, or let them have access to a chart of how you consider them during the production process to ensure the product meets their tastes.

When customers can apparently see that you want the best for them and not just their money, you secure a long-lasting relationship with them.

- **Ask for their opinions**

Virtually everybody loves to be a part of a meaningful process. Let's say you want to change a logo that your customers have been used to for over a decade. It will be totally wrong for you to make the entire process without informing your customers and even asking for their opinion. Right from the moment you think about it and after you have made necessary plans, carry your customers along. To do this, you can make a poll to receive and review their suggestions or opinions.

Welcoming customers' opinions makes them feel recognised and important. If they eventually get to discover that you consider their opinions in the final process, they will value you, and the relationship between you and them will get strengthened.

- **Include them in your plans**

    This is like the previous point except that you may not bring them in, but make plans with them in mind. There is great difference between planning your business and planning your business with your customers in mind. Create a structure to relate with your customers. Consider their business and social life in your plans. Not every time should you talk about them buying from you directly; sometimes, talk about what interest them too.

- **Create an off-business association**

    Think about rewarding your customers with a vacation, free flight ticket, or a dinner with members of your organisation.

This will create strong bonds between you and them, and make you gain more customers who will want to partake in such a reward. Besides, who doesn't like rewards?

Also, this strategy makes your customers want to do more. Everyone likes good thing. So, if there is a target to meet to qualify for such benefit, they will work hard at hitting it.

- **Sales Support**

    You get to your customers through marketing, but for those who will buy a product from you to resell, a simple sales support will go a long way in establishing a great relationship between you and them.

### The Don'ts of Customer Relationship

- Don't be selective in your choice of customers; treat everyone equally regardless of how they look.
- Don't make promises you're not sure of keeping to your customers.
- Avoid over-familiarity that leads to physical touches with your customers. This is a No! No!
- Avoid borrowing money or lending out money to your customers as much as possible. Be professional!

- Never be in an intimate relationship with your customers except he or she is your spouse. Pay attention to this.

### How to Deal with Difficult/Rude/Daring Customers.

### 1) Self-Control:

All controls start with self-control; everyone thinks that dealing with difficult customers is about controlling them; it really starts with controlling yourself. If a customer seems difficult, angry, or possibly abusive, the first attempt is for you to stay calm and even smile if possible. Never argue with a customer. Have you ever seen someone who argues with a customer win?

### 2) Listening:

Another major way to handle difficult customers is by listening. By doing this, you will gather facts, know who the customer is or what he wants. This will definitely make you know how to penetrate through to them and make them agree to your terms and conditions in most cases.

### Main listening skills

**Shutting up:** never miss a good opportunity to listen and do not interrupt while listening.

**Caring:** be there for the customers; show them you care.

**Following:** make sure you engage by using eye contact, uninstructive gestures (such as nodding of your head, saying, or asking very frequent questions).

### 3) Responsiveness:

Willingness to promptly help customers and ability to deliver what you promised dependably and accurately go a long way in helping you handle difficult customers. Also, be supportive and always minimise inconveniences.

## CUSTOMER RETENTION

Customer retention is a process of engaging existing customers to continue buying products or services from your business.

Below are some customer retention techniques you can employ for your business:

- Update them on any new product you have.
- Send random new month messages or seasonal greetings, but keep it brief.
- Ask for reviews when they patronise you.
- Give them guarantee where possible.
- Ensure you send appreciation messages after they pay for goods or services (a short thank you message gives positive vibes).
- Don't give them reasons to forget you after purchase, so make the purchase experience memorable.

## Advantages of Having Competitors

One major advantage of having competitors is that they keep you on your toes. For you to enjoy your customers' patronage and be relevant in the market, your products, services, processes, and promotions must be updated, current, and relevant to the customer at the centre of each move you make.

All products and services have a market. The market comprises customers who pay for the offer and competitors. For a lot of businesses, the competitors are threats; they see competitors as entities that are out there to steal their show.

On the other hand, competitors for some

business owners are completers—people who have required characteristics, skills, and qualities to make the market a better place. Competitors are what you call them, and what you call them will determine how you survive in the business with them.

The market is large, and customers patronise whoever they feel offers them want they want, the way they want it. Only companies who can study, understand, and provide solutions to their problems will have customers' time, money, and trust.

For example, if there is a product only one company produces and, at the same time, has no substitute, the company stands the chance of running the business the way they like. They can set their desired price, appear in market when they like, choose customers to favour, regulate supply at their convenience, or even supply quantities when they should have provided qualities.

Although they make money, they may neither satisfy their customers nor perform at their best.

Competitors make the market innovative and rich. With competitors, you stand chances of operating optimally and giving your customers what they want; since you know there are substitutes for what you offer.

Since competitors are an automatic part of the market, you must operate with your competitors in mind. You need to have a structure that accommodates your competitors and turns their presence to your advantage.

## PERSPECTIVE—COMPLETERS, NOT COMPETITORS

Your perspective of having people in the same industry doing similar things you do will determine your success or failure in business. If you see them as entities that are around to work with you, you will know when to reach out to them and how to remain in the system while retaining your current customers and targeting potential clients.

There is a tendency of being overwhelmed with the presence of competitors that you may misappropriate operations just to level up. You may also want to increase work time, compromise price, neglect collaborations, and give less attention to customer relationship because you are busy trying to prove points. Also, you may not have all the expertise and resources but you can stay on top of the game if you can complement what you have with what others have.

Since we have established that competitors are an inevitable part of the market, there are ways to perceive them that will benefit your business.

- Having competitors increases your efficiency because it helps you perform at your best.

- It makes you think hard and strategically,

thereby leading to creativity.

- Competitors provide reassurance that you are getting your customers because of the quality of products/services you offer.

- It makes your market flexible because you change strategies as customers' behaviours or tastes change.

- It can provide you with distinct advantage from information gotten.

A positive and competitive mindset helps improve delivery in service. It gets every department of a business innovative, leading to high efficiency and profit. With the right mind, there are questions to ask, which if well answered, will turn competitions to your advantage. Ask yourself these: 'Who are my competitors?' 'What do I need to do differently?' 'What do they lack that I can provide?' 'How can I partner or collaborate with them?'

## WHO ARE MY COMPETITORS?

This is one question every successful business individual asks: 'Who are my competitors?' if you can't identify your competitors, you won't know what they are doing right to get the market's attention and what they are probably getting wrong in the market. Understanding what your competitors are doing right can help you improve your service, while also understanding what they do wrong can lead to your area of strength.

For example, Coca-Cola's biggest competitor is Pepsi, but because the Coca-Cola companies know this for a fact, they have been able to come up with varieties and brands that have kept them relevant while their competitors also make profit. There are several ways to identify your competitors. They include:

### 1) Those offering same offer as yours

GLO and MTN are both telecommunications companies offering the same service, so they are competitors. Many people use both services, and will switch to whichever is effective per time. Invariably, this will keep both service providers on their toes, thereby satisfying their customers.

Entities in the market sharing customers who purchase your product are your competitors. If they use same process in production of product or service as yours, then you can't lay claim to customers until you have structures that keep your customers loyal to you for same offer they can get elsewhere. Therefore, ask yourself the question: what customer retention structure do I have in my business?

## 2) Those offering similar products or alternatives that can substitute yours

Fizzy drinks and bottled water companies are offering similar products. Although you can use both to quench thirst despite their differences, their uses are similar. Such companies providing alternatives to your products or services are also your competitors.

Another good example is honey and sugar. They can serve same purpose of sweetening. If your company sells sugar and another company sells well-packaged, affordable honey, the other company is your competitor because if your product isn't available or doesn't meet the customers' tastes anymore, they can easily switch to honey.

## 3) Those whose service can incorporate yours

There are businesses with current operation that can easily switch to what you do or add your service as an extension to theirs. They are also a potential threat—competitors.

## 4) Those who can pay others to produce what you produce or give your offer

There are people who don't have much time to venture into business, but can pay experts to create the market for them. They may decide to invest their money into a current lucrative business which expands the market and increases competitors. Though they are not active but can be, at any instant based on their desires.

## WHAT CAN I DO DIFFERENTLY?

Having competitors should not lead to problems, rather, it should help you to determine how best you are going to reach the market. Below are five ways to answer the question: What can I do differently?

- Determine the market size.
- Determine potential customers.
- Determine your presentation.
- Determine your price.
- Determine mechanism to retain your customers.

### Determine the market size

The market size is the value of your business, competitors, and your current and potential customers. It is how many people patronise the product and/or service that both you and your competitors produce or offer.

To properly handle the competition, you must first have good knowledge about how large the market is—the number of competitors you have to face, the value of customers your competitors have, and the value of customers you think you can attract. If you have estimated value, facts, or figures for these, you can have well-structured plans before going into or continuing with the market. Market size can also help you determine if you have any chances of surviving in the market or not because survival in the market is key!

### Determine Potential Customers

The next step is to determine specifically the number of customers that will buy your product or be willing to take your offer. Of course, this will have to do with how much you can get the market's attention. Your potential customers are those who will do business with you because they have known you in person, have been referred by people who trust you, realise that what you offer solves their problem.

Nobody is ready to change taste if they don't get convinced of a new offer. You must be proactive and up to the task to make them do business with you.

### Determine Your Presentation

In the market, branding and marketing are two key factors that will help you stay aloft irrespective of the competition. How you relate your offer to the market is key to your brand's acceptance. Your name, logo, motto, mission and vision statement, outlets, and accessibility are your presentation to the market.

Customers will patronise you if they get to realise, from your mission, that your offer is better than what they have always been exposed to, or the moment they discover you have the potential to serve them better than those who have been on ground—your competitors.

Research widely and invest money, energy, and time into it. Research if customers love the packaging already in the market or if they would love to welcome a new form or approach. If you get it right, you get the customers.

### Determine the price

Every business individual wants to consider the cost of production before pushing a product to the market at a price comparable to the market price.

Before determining your market price, you need to first research your competitor's prices. By knowing how much your competitors place on a service or product, you can decide how to structure your production process, including man power. It helps you to decide whether to increase the quality of your product at the same price to attract more customers or produce at same quality as others and sell at same range.

### Determine the mechanism to retain customers

It is easy to keep your customers and get more if you know how to retain them. Customers love to be heard and to see that they are a part of the product process. Develop a marketing and sales pattern that keeps your customers coming after doing business with you for the first time.

You can simply create a feedback mechanism using an email list, customer service contact, making a direct call to inquire if your service is appreciated, or have agents who reach out to them either online or physically at scheduled periods.

## HANDLING COMPETITION

As mentioned earlier, it's all about your perspective. In business, a company in the same or similar industry which offers similar product or service is called a competitor; and the presence of one or more competitors can turn out well or bad depending on how you handle it. Here, I will discuss ways to handle the pressure of competition in the market:

1. Make yourself a competitor.
2. Concentrate on customers, not competitors.
3. Offer solutions to problems.

4. Create a great brand.
5. Network with customers and relevant industry giants. You can create your virtual community like Facebook groups, WhatsApp groups, etc.

### Make yourself a competitor:

Isn't it interesting when your competitors are on their toes because you are making a rave in the market? If you want to make yourself a competitor, make your product so rich that customers find it irresistible and prefer it to their initial client's product.

This is going to demand a lot from you. It implies that customers would have known, like, and trusted you. That's is called the KLT factor.

Therefore, it starts from how frequent and consistent you appear in the face and minds of customers, how much they have come to like you personally, and how well they have trusted you to doing business with you and with your claims.

### Concentrate on the customers, not competitors

You are likely to neglect your customers to concentrate on your competitors. However, what matters most isn't the competitors, but customers.

One of the several advantages of market competition is that it allows customers to get quality service in the long run.

The more time you spend understanding your customer's needs and providing solutions, the stronger you become, and the more threat you become to others in your industry over a short period of time.

Giving too much attention to competitors such that you forget your customers are the most important entities in the market, will backfire.

Get necessary information about your competitors, like their prices, how they retain and relate with customers, etc., and then get back to work satisfying your customers.

### Offer solutions to problems

Obviously, everyone wants ease, convenience, or solution to problems they encounter daily. Customers are not sentimental about this; they pay money and commit themselves to clients to help make their lives better and easy to live.

To make your business stand out from the competition, concentrate on solving problems.

Nothing gets customers as fast as they realising there is a new product/service available to ease their stress. As long as you provide affordable solutions, you will have less to bother about your competition because you already created your market.

### Build a great brand

Branding is an important aspect of your presence in the market. With a great brand, you can work your way into the customers' hearts and create a competitive edge. Your brand comprises your business's reputation and personality. Some other times, it may have to do with what is known about your business such as package, logo, and advertisement.

More importantly is customers' perception of your brand. What comes to people's mind the moment they hear your business name or product is called customers' perception and you have to manage it well. If you have a business name or offer a product/service that commands great respect for your commitment to meeting needs, you will have customers recruiting customers for you.

### Network

Networking, sometimes, is about negotiating and bargaining. Your ability to study your competitor's area of weakness and present your strength will improve your overall market experience. Everyone out there can't be your competitor; solely look out for completers too.

Lifefount Hospital provides endoscopy service in the city and enjoys referrals from our competitors who do not offer such service but need them for their patients. In this way, we turned our competitors into our completers. Do you want to know how you can do that in your business, too? Simply ask yourself what you can offer to complete your competitors so you can turn them into completers. You can also leverage their strengths.

There are individuals, organisations, or bodies who would love to work with you for their own benefits and in return help you bring your idea to the market. You must collaborate with such people. You must discover and connect with them. Don't make the mistake of ever underrating any of your competitors. They all have the potential to either kick you out of the market or become your network. The choice is yours to make.

## Chapter Nine

# BUSINESS PLAN

A business plan is a guide or road-map that outlines your business's goals and details on how you plan to achieve those goals.

It is a written document describing the nature of your business, the sales and marketing strategy, and the financial background, which contains a projected profit-and-loss statement.

A business plan is also a document that summarises the operational and financial objectives of a business.

The purpose of a business plan is to identify, describe, and analyse a business opportunity and/or a business already under way while examining its technical, economic, and financial feasibility.

You can't plan where you want your business to be in a few years' time if you don't know where it is now. Before starting your business plan, be sure to conduct a business analysis by using a SWOT (Strengths, Weaknesses, Opportunities, and Threats) analysis.

When doing the analysis section, which is the market, industry, and competitive analysis, you will discuss the opportunities and threats. In your action plan where you discuss people, operations, marketing, and sales, you will discuss the internal analysis of strengths and weaknesses (your business's uniqueness).

An effective business plan must contain several key components that cover various aspects of a company's goals. The important parts of a business plan include:

- Executive summary
- Business description
- Market analysis and strategy
- Marketing and sales plan
- Competitive analysis

- Management and organisation description
- Products and services description
- Operating plan
- Financial projection and needs
- Exhibits and appendices

## 1. Executive summary

The executive summary is the first and one of the most critical parts of a business plan. This summary summarises the business plan and highlights what the business plan will cover. It's often best to write the executive summary lastly so that you have a complete understanding of your plan and can effectively summarise it. Your executive summary should include your organisation's mission statement and the products and services you plan to offer or currently offer. You may also want to include why you are starting the company if the business plan is for a new organisation.

## 2. Business description

The next part of a business plan is the business description. This component describes your business and its goals, products, services, and target customer base. You should also include details regarding the industry your company will serve and any trends or major competitors within the industry. You should also include you and your team's experiences, which comprise your uniqueness in the industry and what sets your company apart from the competition.

## 3. Market analysis and strategy

The purpose of the market analysis and strategy of a business plan is to research and identify a company's primary target audience and where to find this audience. Factors to consider in this section include:

- Where your target market is geographically located.

- The primary pain points experienced by your target customers.

- Your target market's prominent needs and how your products or services can meet these needs.

- The demographics of your target audience.

- Where your target market spends most of their time, such as social media platforms and physical locations.

The goal of this section is to clearly define your target audience so that you can make strategic estimations of how your product or service will perform with this audience.

### 4. Marketing and sales plan

This part of your business plan should cover the specifics of how you plan to market and sell your products and services. The section should include:

- Your intended marketing and promotion strategies.

- Pricing plans for your company's products and services.

- Your strategies for making sales.

- Why your target audiences should purchase from your company versus your competition.

- Your organisation's unique selling proposal.

- How you will get your products and services in front of your target audience.

### 5. Competitive analysis

Your business plan should also include a detailed competitive analysis that clearly outlines a comparison of your organisation to your competitors. Outline your competitors' weaknesses and strengths and how you expect your company to compare to these. This section should also include any advantages your competition has in the marketplace and how you plan to set your company apart. You should also cover what makes your business different from other companies in the industry, as well as any potential issues you may face when entering the marketplace.

## 6. Management and organisation's description

This section of your business plan should cover the details of your business's management and organisation's strategy. Introduce your company's leaders, their qualifications, and responsibilities within your business. You can also include human resources requirements and the legal structure of your company.

## 7. Products and services description

Use this section to further expand on the details of the products and services your company offers, which you covered in the executive summary. Include all relevant information about your products and services, such as how you will manufacture them, how long they will last, what needs they will meet, and how much it will cost to create them.

## 8. Operating plan

This part of your business plan should describe how you plan to run your company. Include information regarding how and where your company will operate, how many employees it will have, and all other pertinent details related to your organisation's operations.

## 9. Financial projection and needs

The financial section of your business plan should detail how you expect to bring in revenue and the funding you'll need to start. You should include your financial statements, an analysis of these statements, and a cash flow projection. Business owners must understand external factors that can affect their businesses' financial viability.

Your business plan must answer some questions like:

- How much money do you need?
- When do you need it?
- Is the cost justified?
- How long will you need the money?
- Do you need collateral for the money?
- What are consumers willing to spend on?

## 10. Exhibits and appendices

The last section of your business plan should include any extra information to support the details outlined in your plan. You can also include exhibits and appendices to support the viability of your business plan and give investors a clear understanding of the research that backs up your plan. Common information to put in this section include:

- Resumes of company management and other stakeholders.
- Marketing research.
- Permits.
- Proposed or current marketing materials.
- Relevant legal documentation.
- Pictures of your product.
- Financial documents.

You can search online for simple templates of a business plan that suits your sector and use it to make yours. If you want to give it to a business consultant to do it for you, ensure you communicate your business effectively to them so the business plan can give you the best roadmap to your business's growth. When you have a business plan, do not keep it away in a locker. It is a living document, therefore visit it regularly to ensure you are on the right track.

## BUSINESS MODEL CANVAS

The Business Model Canvas was proposed by Alexander Osterwalder based on his earlier work on *Business Model Ontology*. It outlines nine segments which form the building blocks for a business model in a nice one-page canvas.

The Business Model Canvas reflects

systematically on your business model so you can focus on your business model segment by segment. This also means you can start with a brain dump, filling out the segments that come to your mind first and then work on the empty segments to close the gaps. The following list with questions will help you brainstorm and compare several variations and ideas for your next business model innovation:

1) **Key Partners**

   Who are your key partners/suppliers?

   What are the motivations for the partnerships?

2) **Key Activities**

   What key activities does your value proposition require?

   What activities are most important in distribution channels, customer relationships, and revenue streams?

3) **Value Proposition**

   What core value do you deliver to the customer?

   Which customers' needs are you satisfying?

4) **Customer Relationship**

What relationship do your target customers expect you to establish?

How can you integrate that into your business in terms of cost and format?

5) **Customer Segment**

Which classes are you creating values for?

Who is your most important customer?

6) **Key Resources**

What key resources does your value proposition require?

What resources are important the most in distribution channels, customer relationships, and revenue stream?

7) **Distribution Channels**

Through which channels do your customers want to be reached?

Which channels work best? How much do they cost? How can they be integrated into your routine and your customers' routines?

### 8) Cost Structure

What are the costs of materials and tools in your business?

Which key resources/ activities are most expensive?

### 9) Revenue Stream

For what value are your customers willing to pay?

What and how do they recently pay? How would they prefer to pay?

How much does revenue stream contribute to the overall revenues?

Business model canvas is a very important one-page document that helps you focus on what is most important in your business processes. You can download it online and make one for your business. Discussing this canvas with your team helps to give clarity to your business model.

**SOURCES OF FUND FOR YOUR BUSIN ESS.**

When you are looking to start or develop a business, you will need some sources of funding. However, figuring out what sources of funding are available to you, as a business owner, is a bit tricky than you think.

Overall, there are two primary forms of financing available to small businesses: debt and equity. There are other types of funding which will help you navigate different sources of funding, the advantages and disadvantages of each funding option, including the stage of business they suit best. The other types of funding are:

**1. Your Personal Savings**

Those who envision going into entrepreneurship can plan and save for a while so they can start small with their money. Some funding opportunities are more accessible to those who can show they invested their money first. It shows that you believe in your enterprise enough to put your personal savings into it.

2. **Friends & Family**

This is one of the commonest ways to access funds, since they trust you. Tell your family and friends about your business plan and show them how you will pay them back. Let them know potential risks and threats that could occur which will help prevent awkward scenarios in case of business failure in the future.

3. **Venture capitalist (VC)**

Venture capitalists invest huge sums into start-ups or expanding businesses with tremendous growth potential and traction, typically investing considerably more capital than angel investors. VCs are professional investors responsible for investing and growing some of the world's most innovative companies, including Facebook, Spotify, and Airbnb.

As with angel investors, there's no obligation to pay back the investment if your start-up fails. Venture capitalists are attractive, as they can offer considerable business knowledge, vast sums of capital, and often take much higher risks.

With higher risk comes the expectation of a higher reward. VCs will expect considerable returns and want a clear exit plan in the form of acquisition or selling shares. These are professional investors, so they'll want to see a solid business plan and sound accounts.

This type of funding is typically reserved for more developed technology businesses. It's often more complicated, as such significant sums of money come with more hands-on investors who will want more control over their investment, and therefore within your business. An entrepreneur who wants total control of his enterprise will not like this funding option.

**4. Creditors/Suppliers**

**5. Angel Investors/Business Angels**

Business angels are private investors, typically former entrepreneurs or wealthy individuals who invest in start-ups and small companies in return for an equity stake of usually 10-20%. Sourcing from business angels is a fantastic way to secure seed money for a project, because they can offer advice, guidance, and mentorship through a project.

Be confident that you can establish a good working relationship with them because you're going to be in business together for a while. Their stake in the project also dictates an amount of control they'll have in the company.

Business angels are helpful, as they are usually willing to take bigger risks than banks. There's also no obligation to pay back the invested capital if the venture flops.

### 6. Traditional Business Loans

Provided you can get them at a reasonable rate, they are still an excellent way to raise finances for your venture, particularly if you are already generating revenue. Remember that any loan is debt finance which you are obliged to pay back (companies like LearnBonds also compare payday loans online). Carefully review any terms you agree to and, when possible, try to find other forms of finance before you consider taking on any debt.

Bank Loans are easily accessible in some countries while very difficult in some because you will be required to bring collateral. This is because banks want assurance of repayment.

Collaterals are assets, personal net worth note such as your house or personal investment which your lender can claim ownership over, if business fails in loan repayment. When requesting loan facility, you must request the amount, state the purpose, and identify expected sales revenue. You will need a business plan which must show cash flow projections, break-even timelines, and profits, to get loans.

Some countries have start-ups loan schemes. The *Start-up Loans Scheme* is a government stimulus package that gives you access to a low-cost loan. The scheme is an excellent way to fund a new venture or expand an existing small business. The loan also comes with 12-months free mentoring, which is invaluable for new entrepreneurs. The entrepreneur, not the company, is liable for this loan.

If you must take a loan, ensure you understand the terms of reference before taking it. This includes interest rate (varies with Central Bank of Nigeria) which increase rates and will affect existing loans or fresh ones, moratorium (if any), repayment plans, monthly repayment, payment holidays, etc.

### 7. Grants (Government and private)

Government and private organisations provide funding and grant opportunities to small businesses. These grants are typically available for new companies or existing businesses who are supporting economic growth in a particular area or nationwide by developing technology in a specific field or helping the disadvantaged.

To be eligible for a small business grant, you must meet the grant-specific criteria. Afterwards, you need to apply and undergo a vetting process. The major benefit of grant funding is that it's effectively free money, which you don't have to pay back.

Sometimes, grants are not the right funding route for your business. Some have very specific eligibility requirements, while some use a very time-consuming application process. Consider whether you can afford to waste the time to apply for a grant, if eventually you weren't selected.

To qualify for grant from donors or government which usually comes with no repayment, your business must be involved in rendering value for community development like the sustainable development goals or government interest. A grant opportunity readily available in Africa is the Tony Elumelu Foundation Grant for entrepreneurs. I was awarded this business grant, which came with mentoring for 12 months, and it validated our business and propelled us in the right direction. In order not to waste time applying, a business owner can use the service of a business consultant to review application before submission.

### 8. Bootstrapping

Bootstrapping is building a company from the ground up with nothing but personal savings, and with luck, the cash coming in from the first sales. The term is also used as a noun: A bootstrap is a business which an entrepreneur with little or no outside cash or other support launches.

Bootstrapping is the minimalistic business culture approach to start a company; it is characterised by extreme sparseness and simplicity. It is one of most effective and inexpensive ways to ensure a business has positive cash flow.

Trade credit (supplier's resources) is one way to maximise your financial resources for the short term. Customer advancement can be used, at the beginning, to reduce the burden of loan which comes with interest. New businesses may have to go into legal agreements before suppliers can release their products since there are no records that you can pay bills on time.

### 9. Incubators/Acceleration Program

Business incubators focus on sectors, technology, and social impact businesses. They provide access to networks that provide training and funds at different development stages like incubation or idea phase, start-up, early phase, growth stage, and mature phase. You can look out for the incubation hubs in your area or beyond. They give many supports like shared office spaces, technology, logistics, mentors, and networks, thereby enabling them to become sustainable and self-sufficient in the long-term.

### 10. Crowdfunding

Crowdfunding platforms allow you to raise funds from a number of small contributions from many investors or purchasers. You can either run an equity-based crowdfunding campaign where you exchange equity for investment or a reward-based crowdfunding campaign where your investors receive perks or rewards in exchange for their capital.

Keep in mind that it usually takes a significant amount of preparation and marketing to create and run a successful crowdfunding campaign. With that in mind, it is an excellent form of alternative finance for small businesses.

### 11. Cooperative Loan

This is a loan at low interest from savings of a group of people in which the borrower is a contributor. It is a win-win mode of funding such that the borrower also gets dividend from the interest paid on the loan. It is also a common source of funding in some parts of Africa.

12. Other sources of income you can look at includes: business credit cards, invoice finance, asset-based lending, hire purchase, finance lease, business competitions, commercial

mortgages, merchant cash advance, and tax reliefs.

## Chapter Ten

# MIND YOUR FINANCES: BOOKKEEPING AND ACCOUNTING PRINCIPLES

Every entrepreneur needs to know his numbers. When you invite a professional to audit your account, there are some basic expectations they have of you. In order to understand how the accounting world works, you need to understand the principles that back what is done so that you can align yourself with these principles for your books to be organised.

When my co-founder and I started Lifefount Hospital, we felt that we will do well because we have medical education but after a year or thereabout, we invited an auditor with excitement to audit our business account.

We used to record our financial details inside a hardcover note, so I handed everything over to the auditor with the account statement, but after glancing through each of them, he pushed all the books back to me and I wondered why.

When I questioned him, he told me he couldn't make sense of our records. I argued that we usually document all the income and expenditures, but in the long run, I realised I had good intentions but no bookkeeping or accounting knowledge. He told me that my bank statement was the only thing that made sense. I felt so embarrassed about his assessment of our performance. Afterwards, I learnt bookkeeping and accounting and used the knowledge to manage our business well.

This incident created a hunger for practical entrepreneurial knowledge in me. While seeking this knowledge, I got a number of suggestions from people to study Business Administration (MBA) but I declined and later found what I was looking for through different programs in Enterprise Development Centre (Lagos Business School), Tony Elumelu Foundation Programme, African

Management Initiative, and Academy for Women Entrepreneurs via Department of Public Affairs, United State Embassy, Nigeria. These and many other programs made me better and I am glad to share my journey and experiences with you.

It's okay if your account is a mess now, but it shouldn't be after reading this book. It's important for all businesses to keep track of their financial statements and ensure that they are correctly and efficiently drawn up.

Even though it's your business, you still need a third-party scrutiny which would enable others to know what you are doing, how you are doing it, and what you need to do. If you want to go far, you have to involve other professionals and some of your management staff.

Proper bookkeeping and accounting help ensure a third-party comprehends your financial state.

### BOOKKEEPING

Bookkeeping is the recording of all financial transactions. It is also the process of rightly capturing the effect of all financial transactions including purchases, sales, receipts, and payments by an individual person or an organisation/corporation in a form that it's easy to determine if your business is making profit or running at a loss.

It is the foundation of accounting in a business that feeds other accounting processes. For a business account to be right, you must do your bookkeeping right.

It is also part of the processes of accounting in business. There is a misconception that you should only keep records for cash transactions. Well, do bookkeeping anytime any transaction is being carried out, either paid or unpaid.

One of the principles of accounting is consistency. Be consistent in recording your transactions, either purchases or sales.

The reason you got into a financial muddle was because you didn't keep your books up to date. You must be consistent with it. If you can't, you have to get someone to assist you, depending on how big your transactions or company is, but you need to know what you are required to do.

Write policies to ensure that your employees record transactions consistently so that you will not be in a mess.

Nine out of ten businesses fail because of poor financial management. In order not to join that statistics, make up your mind to learn about bookkeeping and accounting practices as doing this will make your business grow and do well.

There is a limit to the amount of transactions that you can remember after a while if you do not record it appropriately and promptly. It is important for business owners to open a business bank account. You must separate personal money from business money. Lodge in your income and do your expenses with correct narration. This is helpful in preparing your business financial statement and auditing. It also helps in attracting investors and in knowing your business growth.

Let's take a tour of the benefits of bookkeeping.

## BENEFITS OF BOOKKEEPING

### 1. Bookkeeping helps you prepare a budget:

Many business owners go into a lot of stress in running their businesses, but when you, as a business owner, do your record keeping appropriately, you will notice some patterns in your business and also budget for those different times.

For example, if you sell bottled water, you will notice that you sell a lot during hot seasons. Therefore, you must ensure that you have enough money with miscellaneous to produce more water to sell in that season during the coming year.

It's only when you keep appropriate account that you will notice trends in your business. This helps you to prepare a budget for the coming year.

A proper bookkeeping helps you keep budgets. When income and expenses are properly organised, it makes it easier to review financial resources and expenses, and also helps with your cash flow forecast, thereby keeping your budget appropriately.

## 2. Bookkeeping helps you with tax preparation.

You can make the tax filing process more efficient by having a bookkeeping function within your company. Bookkeeping is important for filing your personal tax returns tools. That is, when you keep your record appropriately, consistently, and timely, it helps you in tax preparation.

Keeping your records properly is one of the

requirements for having a business because the tax collectors will require tax from you but if you have the right records, you can show them a proof of the exact amount of tax you are supposed to pay, but if you don't keep your records appropriately, you will be under the obligation to pay any amount you are given. At the end of the day, it's costlier not to keep a book record.

### 3. Bookkeeping gives your business an organisational outlook.

Another benefit of bookkeeping is that it helps your business to have an organised outlook. Being organised is a skill every business owner should have because few parties are interested in your company's financial records: the IRS, investors employees, lenders, and the government.

Many people struggle to work in banks or some other big companies, but they don't want to work in SMEs because they don't know that some of them pay better than big organisations. Another reason is because most SMEs are not organised. Everybody wants an organised life, so dear entrepreneur, you need to organise your business.

Many people are interested in your business's financial record and revenue system because they want to collect money. If you keep it right, you can chase them off your back, pay what is appropriate, and they cannot get more than that from you.

Your employees are also interested in your financial records. When COVID-19 struck, our business could not make enough money, people were afraid to come into a hospital space because of the risk of infection. At the end of a month, we could not make enough money to pay our employees. Since we had appropriate records, our employees knew we didn't make enough revenue, so they accepted their salaries in two instalments.

Our employees trusted us because we have an appropriate accounting and bookkeeping system, so they accepted the plan to be paid in instalments.

It is to your benefit in so many ways when you do bookkeeping right.

Customers also want to know that you have appropriate record keeping. Our company lost six million naira to our debtors who defaulted and we couldn't pursue the recovery because we lacked proper bookkeeping process. Our customers knew we were not keeping proper records, which made them escape with our money. Eventually, we incurred a loss because of a lack of appropriate bookkeeping.

### 4. Bookkeeping helps in better decision making

In the year 2015, an investment company in USA approached me, saying they were ready to invest in African businesses with about ten million US dollars ($10, 000, 000) but angry that African investors usually ask for small money whenever they approach them that they want to invest in them. I was at the point of signing a non-disclosure with them on behalf of our company but I had to withdraw because we didn't have all the records they requested for.

You could be standing in the way of your business's progress by not keeping appropriate books in your company. Investors are interested in your business and when you want to expand your business but need more cash, lenders also get interested in your bookkeeping.

The benefits of bookkeeping are enormous. You cannot do well in your business without doing appropriate bookkeeping. Your sector, however, is not an excuse for you not to do appropriate bookkeeping.

Even if you own a big organisation, you can only supervise your staff if you know these things. Many companies failed because the management didn't know anything about bookkeeping. You don't have to be a chartered accountant to know and apply basic principles.

## 5. Bookkeeping Is Good for Audit Purposes

You will be able to audit your business account at the end of each year if you do appropriate bookkeeping.

Bookkeeping also helps you to detect and correct errors. Don't lose money because of a lack of appropriate financial management and bookkeeping. Sometimes ago, we discovered that ten thousand naira came into our account but instead of our bank account to increase by that amount, the previous balance reduced by two thousand naira. If we were not doing appropriate bookkeeping, we would not have been able to write a letter and trace the money.

It's easier to plan when you keep your records right. You must also do it instantly because you can forget. Don't wait till the next day. You have to monitor every transaction. It helps you to get faster response when you make demands. When we wrote a letter to the bank, they sorted the issue immediately because we kept appropriate records.

Bookkeeping also helps in making faster financial analysis. We can say, within a snap of a finger, the amount we made in January, February, and every month of the year.

Samsung started as a very small business selling groceries like milk and sugar, but it has become a global brand today. Could it be that the business you underrate always is a global brand?

Bookkeeping helps you to be compliant with the law. It helps you with budgeting and when you need a loan, you will be able to get it quickly.

I was able to partake in the loan which the federal government of Nigeria gave to businesses during the pandemic. It came into my business at the right time because I needed to service an equipment in our hospital, which was over a million naira with other projects that we were doing.

This loan came in at the right time, but the reason we could ask for it was because we were ready. One of the things they requested for was three years auditing report. Confidence came from the fact that we were doing the right thing, so I applied and we got it.

The reason your business is not growing is not

because someone is not helping you or giving you money, but because you have refused to do appropriate bookkeeping and you lack the confidence to approach opportunities that God has put in the way to help your business. Therefore, decide to change now; business is war, but you must learn before you earn.

*Self-made* is a movie on Netflix and a good enterprise story line which I would love to recommend for you to watch.

## CASH FLOW

To have a business, you must have cash flowing in and out of your enterprise; you cannot be cash trapped. Hence, it's important you plan so you can run your business smoothly. This takes us to cash flow projection.

Cash flow analysis keeps you from going out of business. Many businesses with great profit margin go out of business because of cash flow shortages; they do not have cash to pay their bills.

With cash flow projection you will know how much money goes in and out of your business and how much you have left at the end of a particular period either daily, monthly, quarterly, or annually.

## Steps to Creating Cash Flow Projections

1. Start with the amount of cash at the beginning of a period.

2. Add all cash payments you expect to be paid for your sales.

3. Subtract all amounts you expect to spend, including staff salary.

4. The balance over the designated period is a cash balance projection.

## Advantages of Cash Flow Projection

Cash flow projection helps a business owner to have an idea if there will be enough cash to pay all the people working for him and other expenses that are important to keep the business running. If the projection shows that the business cannot run on the cash balance, then the business owner will have to look for other sources like loans or delay payments of vendor so the business can survive.

You can inject cash as a business owner which can increase your equity or recorded as loan in your management account. Loans (at an interest rate as fair and as you decide) must come with a loan agreement form duly filled and signed with witnesses' signatures. When your business is stable and able, you can make the loan repayment, which must enter the management record too.

Kindly record it anytime you do cash drawings in your management account.

**SALES:** Sales are recorded whenever products or services get to the customer, irrespective of payment or not.

**RECEIVABLES:** Receivables are the balance of payment yet to be received from a customer who already received product or service.

**PROFIT:** Profit is the balance left from your sales after deducting all business expenses. Please note: not personal expenses.

You must decide and document the mode of payment and tools or instrument that are suitable for you.

## How to Track Your Business's Position Using Basic Bookkeeping

1. Record all transactions immediately using necessary documents like profoma invoice, sales invoices, receipts, credit note, debit note, requisition forms, stock keeping, payables, receivables, taxes, loans, etc.

2. Categorise them into income and expenditure using your ledger and or an accounting software package (offline and cloud base).

3. Take stock of your inventory by doing a physical count and valuation, timely. It could be daily, weekly, monthly, quarterly, or annually.

4. Have a depreciation schedule for your asset, i.e., things you use for one year and above, which brings in economic benefit to the business.

5. Prepare your income statement monthly, showing your receipts, expenses, accounts receivables, payables, etc.

6. Be familiar with necessary information such as your payables, receivables, and customer balances. Accounting software can make this easier.

## Five Tips on How to Separate Personal Finance from Business Finance

a) **Maintain a separate bank account:**

Make sure you have a separate account for business and personal purpose. Note that according to business entity principle, you are a different person from your business and you must never make mistakes of spending from your business without recording and replacing it.

Also note that anytime you loan money to your business, you must record appropriately and promptly. You can loan at an interest and pay back accordingly. Director or management account comes into play here.

b) **Keep proper and timely transaction records:**

If you delay in recording your transaction at the right place, you can forget about it later, so do it now.

c) **Pay yourself a salary:**

When I became a full-time entrepreneur, my business could only afford to pay me a salary of about 25% of what I earned as a government worker, but we grew from there. It could be small and you may have to take a loan to achieve this; just keep your records as you focus on improving the value you bring to people. Doing this will make your business grow profits and be sustainable. You can grow organically without external funding, but for major expansion, equity or loan may help your business grow faster.

d) **Track your expenses:**

For micro businesses that run their petty cash from a purse, you can put the money and pen in an envelope such that at every expenditure, you can write it on the envelope immediately and transfer into your record book later in the day; or you record on your accounting software immediately.

e) **Hire an accountant:**

You can hire a part-time accountant or leverage friends who are professionals. If you can afford a full-time accountant, get it because as you grow, you will definitely need a professional to handle your account.

f) **Audit your account:**

You can use a part-time or full-time auditor to achieve this. You can also use external auditors for your yearly audit and tax filing.

Although laws differ from country to country, you need an audit of the financial statements of a public company for government contract, investment, financing, and tax purposes. Independent accountants or auditing firms can perform the auditing for you. Results of the audit are summarised in an audit report that either provides an unqualified opinion on the financial statements or qualifications as to its fairness and accuracy.

The audit opinion on the financial statements is usually included in the annual report.

### Disadvantages of An Inappropriate Bookkeeping System

- Confusion on the financial state of the business.
- Inability to track your debtors.
- Inability to get access to finance from standard creditors and financial institutions.
- Inability to predict the going concern of the business.
- Loss of investor's money.

Financial statements (or financial reports) are formal records of the financial activities and position of a business, person, or other entity.

Relevant financial information is presented in

a structured manner and in a form, which is easy to understand. It typically includes four basic financial statements accompanied by a management discussion and analysis:

- A balance sheet or statement of financial position
- Reports on a company's assets
- Liabilities
- Owners' equity at a given point in time

An income statement (profit or loss report, statement of comprehensive income, or statement of revenue and expenses) reports on a company's income, expenses, and profits over a stated period. A profit or loss statement provides information on the operation of the enterprise. These include sales and the various expenses incurred during the stated period.

A statement of changes in equity or equity statement, or statement of retained earnings reports on the changes in equity of the company, over a stated period.

A cash flow statement reports on a company's cash flow activities, particularly its operating, investing, and financing activities, over a stated period.

Notably, a statement of financial position represents a single point in time, where the income statement, the statement of changes in equity, and the cash flow statement each represent activities over a stated period.

For large corporations, these statements may be complex and may include an extensive set of footnotes to the financial statements and management discussion and analysis. The notes typically describe each item on the balance sheet, income statement, and cash flow statement in details. Notes to financial statements are considered an integral part of the financial statements (Source: Wikipedia).

## Uses of Financial Statements

Owners and managers require financial statements to make important business decisions that affect the business's continued operations. Financial analysis is then performed on these statements to provide management with a more detailed understanding of the figures. These statements are also used as part of management's annual report to the stockholders.

Prospective investors make use of financial statements to assess the viability of investing in a business. Investors often use financial analysis while professionals (financial analysts) prepare them, thus providing investors with the basis for making investment decisions.

Financial institutions (banks and other lending companies) use them to decide whether to grant a company with fresh working capital or extend debt securities (such as a long-term bank loan or debentures) to finance expansion and other significant expenditures.

Employees also need these reports in making collective bargaining agreements (CBA) with the management in the case of labour unions or in discussing their compensation, promotion, and rankings.

## ACCOUNTING PRINCIPLES AND STANDARDS

There are certain principles and standards that should guide your accounting operations, leading us to the next sub-topic.

Accounting principles are rules and guidelines that companies must follow when reporting financial data. Accounting standards, however, are procedures that explain the basis of financial accounting policies and practices.

Accounting principles serve as a significant purpose of standardising how businesses perform their financial reporting activity.

## THE PRINCIPLE OF BUSINESS ENTITY

This is a concept that states that a business is an entity itself and it should be treated as a separate person, which differs from its owner.

Know that your business is separate from you. You are not your business and your business is not you. Avoid drawing from the business and ensure you put yourself on a salary. You know the weight of your business; therefore, this should determine the amount you pay yourself on a monthly basis.

If your business cannot pay you a million naira in a month, don't request for it from your business.

If you choose a fair salary and your business cannot still pay you at the moment, have an appropriate record to note that.

Also, have a bank account for your business in your business name so that you will be able to partake in business opportunities.

Finally, record all the affairs in your business and avoid personal affairs. You cannot pay your children's school fees from your business account. Don't kill your business; the world wants it to survive. Every personal and philanthropist expenses you want to do should be done from your salary, not from the business.

## THE PRINCIPLE OF GOING CONCERN

The going concern principle is the assumption that a business will continue to exist in the near future and will not liquidate or be forced out of business. This means that accounting is hopeful for your business's survival, so you should be hopeful too.

When an accounting principle hopes that your business will not die, you, as the business owner, must have a greater faith and do all it takes for the business to survive.

In the same vein, if a business owner can know when a business is dead, you should know when to end it or take a break and re-strategise.

You must know when to let go or take a proper break to withdraw, retreat, and take honest assessment of yourself and your business. Know where you fell short, or employ a business management consultant to assist you so that you will not make the same mistake again when you start another business.

Albert Einstein said, 'Insanity is doing the same thing over and over again and expecting different results.'

As a business owner, you need to understand your going concern.

Do a SWOT Analysis of your business to know what the Strengths, Weaknesses, Opportunities, and Threats are or the risks that are involved.

The going concern principle serves as a guideline which allows readers of a business's financial statement to assume that the business will continue to operate long enough to carry out its current obligations, objectives, and commitments.

It's a living statement or a true assessment of your business that is usually written in your audited financial statement where you and your investors can read from. This means that you must audit your business.

Do you know your turnover in the past 3 years?

If you can't say, it means that you need to pay attention to your business accounting and bookkeeping from this month onward.

You will have the true statement of what transpired if you are able to audit your business at the end of the year. Don't trivialise your business. Size does not attract investors to businesses but having a good structure and doing well does.

### ACCRUAL CONCEPT

This is a very important concept that you need to understand in business. It is what makes your business to be organised and the basic thing about it is that you will record sales when you give an invoice to your customer, not when cash is received.

This is the most fundamental principles of accounting which requires recording revenues when they are earned and not when they are received in cash.

You will record sales when someone orders for your goods. When you make expenses, you won't also wait to pay the cash before you record.

For example, when you buy goods in bulk, you might not be able to make immediate payment, but it must be recorded immediately that goods have been purchased even if money has not been paid.

Also, if sales are made, it must be recorded immediately even if you have not received cash.

## COST CONCEPT

Cost concept states that you should record all acquisition of items, such as assets or things needed for expending, in the book as cost, except it is stated otherwise. For example, if you buy a building for five million naira, record it like that.

## CONSISTENCY CONCEPT

The concept of consistency means that accounting method, once adopted, must be applied consistently in the future. If for any valid reason the accounting policy is changed, a business must disclose the nature of change, the reason for the change, and the effect on the item of financial statement.

The basic principle of financial statement states that the same method for doing account should be used from one financial year to the next so that profit, loss, etc., can be compared.

Consistency in accounting is, therefore, *key*.

## Chapter Eleven

# MIND YOUR FINANCES: CLASSIFICATION OF ACCOUNT

*Before reading this chapter, get a writing material to document what you are going to stop, start, and continue in your business from the knowledge you get from this chapter.*

Every business owner must have a basic accounting knowledge so that they can employ an accountant or auditor once the business gets bigger beyond what they or an amateur can do.

This knowledge will help you know what to ask the accountant or auditor and control the service they are rendering for you.

Whenever you employ an auditor to vet your account, they will make their observation known to you when they are done; but if you are a total novice in accounting, you may not take those corrections or feedback and use them for your business's progress.

After keeping your business's record as learned in bookkeeping, you must organise it into accounts. There are several accounts you can keep in a business, but I'll share four of them with you:

- Asset account
- Liability account
- Income account
- Expense account

### Asset Account

An asset is a resource that is owned or controlled by a company which can be used to provide a future economic benefit. In other words, assets are items that a company uses to generate future revenues or maintain its operation. They are the things that your company owns or are controlled by your company in which you can use to provide future economic benefits.

Based on duration, we can classify assets into:

- Current asset
- Non-current asset

Current asset has a useful life of one year or less, *while* non-current asset has longer than one-year useful life.

Current assets are inventories, raw material, and other things in your store. They are cash from your income, the money you have in your bank account that you have access to, and your receivables, which is the money for the service you rendered to someone or product you sold that you are yet to be paid for. Remember to issue an invoice and do not write a receipt for it until they pay you. Those resources are yours even though you are yet to get them.

Non-current assets are lands, buildings, plants, machineries and equipment, motor vehicles, computer, furniture, etc. They are called non-current assets because the value for each is more than one year.

## Liability Account

Liability account is a general ledger account in which a company records its debt, customer's deposit, customer's prepayment, and certain deferred income taxes. This is where you record the amounts of money you owe people.

Examples of items you have in your liability account are the *current* and *non-current liability*.

Current liabilities are liabilities that you have to pay back in less than a year, e.g., payables (having to pay vendors immediately they supply you can be financially stressful for your company. You must have a written policy that guides your business. For example, when you receive a supply, you can have a policy that pays once in a month, twice a month, or every three months so that you can have some peace of mind rather than having vendors disturb you frequently), bank overdraft or current liability, Short-termloans, Income tax payable (you need to pay your taxes according to the financial act that guides every business), and Interest payable (banks' interests are charged annually so, pay this back.)

Non-current liabilities are liabilities that take you more than a year to pay back, e.g., long-term liability bond payable, long-term lease, and deferred tax (the tax you are supposed to pay this year which you deferred till another year).

## Expense Account

Expenses are the costs incurred to generate revenues. In other words, a firm records an expense when it disburses cash or promises to disburse cash for an asset or service used to generate income.

These are your frequently incurred expenses, e.g., stationeries (used to type letters), fuel, wages, salaries, etc. These will be recorded under expense account.

## Income Account

Income account is where you record all the income or revenue you get from your business, i.e., all the activities and transactions that bring in money into your business.

There are many other accounts apart from the four we mentioned, like withdrawal account, capital account, etc.

## PETTY CASH ACCOUNT

This topic is very dear to my heart because I'm an advocate of peace in the enterprise. I believe that your business should bring you peace and joy, not headache; but for most business owners, especially the small enterprises, they have a lot of headaches because they don't know what to do.

To ensure that everything works, they overwork and micromanage. At the end of it all, they get tired. I want to believe that after reading this book, you will be a better entrepreneur who knows what to do and how to do it. Therefore, let's talk about *Petty Cash Account.*

## PETTY CASH:

This is a small amount of cash that is kept on the company premises to pay for minor cash needs. It is used to cover daily expenses, i.e., a petty cash account that takes care of the daily expenses in your company. If you have to be the one to give your workers money for everything they need each day, e.g., ink, tape etc., you will wear yourself out and your workers will think that you don't trust them. This will eventually give you a lot of headaches.

You won't be able to travel or take up higher functions that are supposed to be the work of a CEO because this is going to clog your mind while you are doing the nitty gritty of daily work, which is not supposed to be.

Instead, have a petty cash account that you will put a certain amount in which your cashier, accountant, or a designated staff will handle while he gives you feedback as and at when due.

You may want to ask: how much should I give for my petty cash? Well, you know what your transactions are like and the limit you want to put to it per time, therefore; you control the policy of what goes into it and the time.

You must experiment and monitor petty cash for a specific period before you establish a fixed amount as float which can be reviewed when the need arises. For example, if you spend about twenty thousand naira on different things that you need to run your company per week, you can decide to keep your float at twenty thousand naira per week.

Don't keep sending in the float at the end of every week. Get feedback on how the money was spent, which the petty cash account contains.

When you send money from your cash account to petty cash, it's called a float. This is the money you credit your petty cash account from your cash account and as you send it in, whoever receives it must record and fill a payment voucher to show that he received the money.

This is a sample or template of a petty cash account you can use or modify.

## PETTY CASH BOOK

| Total Receipts | Cash Book Folio | Date | Particulars | Voucher No. | Total Payments | Postage & Telegrams | Cleaning | Stationery | Traveling Expenses | Misc. Expenses | Ledger | Ledger Folio |
|---|---|---|---|---|---|---|---|---|---|---|---|---|
| | | | | | | | | | | | | |
| | | | | | | | | | | | | |
| | | | | | | | | | | | | |
| | | | | | | | | | | | | |
| | | | | | | | | | | | | |
| | | | | | | | | | | | | |
| | | | | | | | | | | | | |
| | | | | | | | | | | | | |
| | | | | | | | | | | | | |
| | | | | | | | | | | | | |

It's from this petty cash that your designated staff or cashier can spend from so they won't have to come to you when they want to buy any little thing in the company. With this, you will have time for higher functions on creativity, strategy, and the way to move the business forward.

You also won't have to bother yourself on every little thing in the company. They will have to record everything they spend the money on and have receipts for each purchase to ensure proper documentation.

The receipts give you the right understanding of the type of document you need to fill for proper bookkeeping and accounting. They serve as third-party evidence so that you will have an adequate understanding of your account.

When you experiment, for example, with twenty thousand naira and you realise they are requesting for more every two days, you may have to increase it to like a hundred thousand naira so you can reduce the frequency of sending in the float.

Don't forget that you need to monitor the petty cash account even though you are not the one spending the float.

There was a time our accountant sent in the

report of the petty cash account that was spent for a week in order to get the float for the following week and I noticed that they spent more on an item than regular so I asked a question: why are you spending so much on this thing? I got a detailed explanation and immediately, they got another float.

If you are the one in charge of giving out money every time the company needs an item, then you won't have the time to provide strategic leadership to the business.

Experiment to know the amount to give and also monitor to know how long it takes them to spend a particular amount of money. This will allow you to establish a fixed amount as float that can be reviewed whenever you think it should.

## IMPREST SYSTEM

An imprest system is a process of reimbursing the petty cash account. The money that goes into the petty cash account is called *float,* but when you reimburse it, it's called an *imprest system*. Imprest is very important in business.

## TYPES OF IMPREST ACCOUNT

The imprest account is of two types:

- **Standing imprest:** When a float is given throughout a financial year.

- **Special advance:** An imprest that is specific for a project. You can give petty cash account that will be used to run the business from time to time in a year. It could be specifically for a project.

In 2019, we had a project of screening the breast of women, doing breast examination ultrasound, and mammography. We gave a special float for this particular project and we were to give a feedback in report of how it was spent.

An imprest could be the one you use regularly for your business or a particular one assigned for your project, which could be a building project or any other project.

### Advantages of Petty Cash Account

1. It encourages division of labour.

   Many times, we have capable hands around us but we do not know because we do not give them responsibilities to do, but when you operate a petty cash account, you have an opportunity to allow one of your employees express himself to show that he is responsible. At that point, you will be able to focus on higher functions while he will be assigned or appointed to concentrate on that task and in that way, you will be able to have division of labour rather than you being a jack of all trade; doing everything, from gateman to cashier to production manager to quality control, etc.

2. It makes comparison of the petty expense between two periods possible.

Like I said earlier about the report of a petty cash account that was once given to me, I compared it with the previous weeks, noticed about 200% increase on the money spent on a particular item, and asked questions before approving another impress for the petty cash.

Petty cash account helps you compare and also gives your employees the impression that you are a boss who pays attention to details, is observant, and has control over what they do. Meanwhile, when you don't know because there are too much data for you to process especially the tiny ones that is not supposed to be your responsibility, you will not make head or tail of the whole thing; your account will be a mess and you won't know when to say *stop*, *start*, or *pause*.

Your employees will begin to feel that you are not in charge, but when you sit as a CEO and you're able to look at things and notice the differences in them, then they will begin to see you as the CEO that you are. That makes me buttress the fact that being a CEO is much more than just having a company of your own. It's a responsibility and this is how you get to do it in a very organised way.

3. It helps in controlling such petty expenses more effectively.

This is where policing, one of the 4Ps of system mentioned in the Yemisi Adeyeye's Quadrant, comes in. Control is another word for policing. You will be able to police your account better when you sit at the top to look at it well instead of being muddled up in the daily and tiny details of spending.

4. It makes the main cash book more organised, informative, clean, and clear by including only major transactions.

This is where you can find fuel (petrol), generator, engine oil, spring and some other tiny details of generator but when you are transferring it from the petty cash account into your expenses account, it's going to be under a major heading: *generator expenses*. If someone wants to know the breakdown of the generator expenses, they will come into the petty cash account to know what the details are because that is the account that accommodates every expense.

When you want to take it to a bigger account which is the expense account or your cash book, you will notice you do not need to include those tiny details. Instead, it will come in as *generator expense* such that you, as the business owner or CEO, can access the amount that was spent on a particular project during the previous month and then compare it with that of the current month. You will be able to ask questions, make strategic plans, and give instruction or direct their activities.

5. It saves time because inside the cash book; you don't have to post the nitty gritty of each payment, instead, you will post as a particular head.

You can only be recognised as an entrepreneur, get grants and loans, be exposed to other opportunities, and also mentor others easily when you do things right, as stated in this book. You may not do all the accounting yourself but as a business owner, you need to have the basic knowledge which is what you are going to get from this book so that by the time you have expanded enough to get an accountant and employ someone that is knowledgeable, you can speak their language. When they communicate, correct, or advise you, you will understand and be able to flow along with them while developing your business.

There are many opportunities I've benefitted from, and the major thing I did to access them was to gain the knowledge, practise them in my business, and go for opportunities. When you learn, it's easier to earn. To be successful, you must be intentional. If there is anything you need to learn, please go for knowledge. It is now accessible than ever before.

Whenever a transaction takes place, there must be a third-party evidence like payment vouchers, receipts, invoices, petty cash books, etc. They are the things that make your business accounting organised. **Wave software** is a free software you can use for accounting in business, but it is technical to use.

### SOURCE DOCUMENTS

A source document is an original document that contains the details of a business transaction. It captures the key information about a transaction.

A source document contains the following information:

- Names of the parties involved
- A description of business transaction
- The date of the transaction
- The specific amount of money that was involved in the transaction
- An authorising signature and/or that of the other part involved in the transaction

Examples of source documents and related business transactions that appear in the financial record are:

- Bank statement
- Cash receipt
- Credit card receipts
- Customer's invoice
- Supplier's invoices
- Purchase orders
- Time cards
- Requisition forms
- Cancelled checks

- Cheques
- Petty cash vouchers
- Payment vouchers
- Debit notes
- Payment notes
- Pay in slip, etc.

These are examples of source documents that your company should have.

When you are doing any transaction in your business, apart from the person giving out the money or recording those things in a particular account, there should be other documents where the person who received them can also put his signature attesting to it that the transaction happened.

When you want to do your business auditing at the end of the year, all these source documents will be reviewed, which is what the accountant or cashier in charge of your accounting recorded.

Apart from you recording your transaction in a ledger, excel document, accounting software, etc., there must also be another document that supports the transaction's existence. That document serves as a third-party evidence.

When you want to give out the money to the

cashier, you must fill the payment voucher and the recipient too must sign and write that he got that money through whatever means you used to pay. If it's a cheque, you'll make a photocopy and add to it. The essence of the source document is that there should be evidence that the transaction happened apart from the one you have recorded.

For example, you sent someone to a place to run company errands and there was no receipt for that transportation from point A to point B. The petty cash voucher would stand as an evidence that money was spent; that way, it will be recorded that there was transportation from point A to point B at XYZ amount.

According to accounting procedure, there must be receipt for every transaction but if there was no receipt or invoice to back it up, make sure the petty cash voucher is filled, that is going to serve as a source document for how the money in the petty cash account was spent.

## Bank Statement

This is a document gotten from the bank showing all the transactions that transpired between your organisation and the bank. It is another type of source document which is a third-party evidence. As a business owner, you and your accountant or cashier who is in charge of bookkeeping know that the company is making money but you need a third-party evidence to prove that you actually have that turnover which is why every business owner is encouraged to open a business bank account and ensure that all your sales goes through the bank so that the bank can stand as an evidence to attest to it that you have that exact turn over in a year.

If you want to be called a proper entrepreneur or want your business to grow, everything about your business cannot start and end with you. If you want to be proud of your business and want it to exist for a long time, others must be involved, one of which is the *bank*.

You must register your business and have a bank account in your business name. These are the processes you have to put in place to make your business to grow.

Your bank statement is very important, with the

bank serving as another corporate entity that knows about your business.

## Invoices

This is an order to pay. It is an evidence that someone owes you, so when you receive an invoice from someone, the person is telling you that you owe him. When goods and services are rendered, you must give invoices.

Invoice is also an evidence which shows you made a sale. Sale is not cash; it simply means that you rendered a service or sold a product to a customer.

Sometimes, the payment comes immediately the goods and services are being rendered so you can order invoices first and, at the same time, order receipt when they pay.

## Cash Receipts

Receipt is a document that proves that money has been paid for a transaction rendered. You give this when a customer pays you. Sometimes, stock keepers don't know the difference between invoices and receipts. They sometimes give an invoice (which is an instruction that you are going to pay them) after payment, instead of giving a receipt. You must have both invoices and receipts and issue them at the right time.

An example is in the education sector, when your students resume newly at the beginning of a term, you are supposed to send all of them invoices because it means that they owe you money. You state the amount in the invoice, and when they pay, you issue out receipts.

What if someone already pays before the term begins?

In a case like this, as you receive the money, give both the invoice and receipt together. It could be at different or same times for those who pay at once.

### Time Cards

These are also source documents that show when your employees resume or leave work, the number of days they come in a month, etc. This helps you calculate how much time they've invested in your business versus the number of times you agreed. This will determine if you are to give them the amount you have agreed to pay on a monthly basis, or less or more.

Time cards are very important, especially for those who are into production whose staff don't come to work frequently. This will help you with your accounting as you will be sure of the duration each staff spent in production, so that you can calculate their money accordingly. This way, you will not be over paying them or paying them for what they never did. Instead of cards, we now have devices they can use to log in and out such that at the end of the month you will make analysis. You can use whatever works for you, but know that they also influence your account.

The entire documents I've mentioned have templates. Kindly search online for suitable templates of source documents.

### Requisition form

This is a document used to make a request to purchase an item for any department in an organisation. When you or one of your employees wants to buy something that the petty cash does not cover for, how do they make the requisition? Through a requisition form.

As a business owner you must remember that your responsibility is to make policies work. It is not a one-time thing; you need to keep developing your processes and improving on your policies and strategies.

If someone needs to buy something that the petty cash does

not cover for, there must be a requisition form answering the following questions:

- Who is requesting for this?
- Which department needs it?
- What do they need it for?
- What date and time are they making this request?
- When is the time they really need it?

That's because all these information help you prioritise the necessities in your company per time so you will not buy unnecessary things while a genuine need is pending. Develop a requisition form and teach your staff how to make use of it or give important information on who makes the requisition.

Our company's heads of departments fill the requisition form for their departments. If you want each of your staff to make requisition, make sure you document your processes and follow it.

Requisition helps you know who is requesting for something and how to plan for its provision. If you observe that a particular request is of topmost priority, you can get a quotation from your suppliers and choose the one you feel suits you. Afterwards, you can approve the purchase. You can also release funds or defer payment depending on your policy on vendor payment. Some pay once a week, while some companies' policies state that you pay vendors every two months.

## Cancelled Cheques

You may be wondering why you need to keep it since you didn't use it. Please do not tear your cancelled cheques. If you authorise a cheque and you noticed it's no longer necessary or something happens, just draw two or three lines across the cheque and keep that cheque in your cheque book. Look for a stapler and staple it back to where it should be in your cheque book because this is evidence that something happened. The essence is for you to be able to account for every cheque.

If you have documented it in the payment voucher, you can make a copy and staple it with the payment voucher to state that although you issued it, you did not use it.

This also helps you to prevent fraud. By the time your company gets bigger and you are no longer in charge of this daily activities, you now have financial department to monitor them, all these policies and products will make it impossible for people to defraud you because they know that everything will be queried.

## Cheques

This is an instruction to the bank to pay a certain amount of money. Cheques are also source documents. As you issue out cheques, it means that the money you are transferring is coming from your cash account. You need to take a photocopy of it and staple it with the payment voucher while the person who will receive the money will fill the payment voucher and go with the cheque to use. It helps you to know how the cheque went and what cause it went for.

It will also save you the argument of the company getting the cheque or not and the exact person who came to receive it. This proper policy and process on how to give out and pick up cheques will save you all the confusion. The person who picks up the cheque will sign and you will have a copy of the cheque too, to be saved somewhere.

## Credit Note

It's a document issued to a customer when goods are returned or services were not rendered. It is also issued when there are damages on products, or when there is over-payment, or mistake on the price of original invoice.

If for example, you ordered for 100 bags of potatoes but observed that 10 out of them were bad, you cannot sell the rotten potatoes.

After you counting and telling the salesman that you want to return the 10 bags that are not good for sale, don't just return those bags of potatoes, instead, ensure you get a credit note stating that they are going to credit you for the money of those bags or replace the bags of potatoes.

### Pay-in slip

This is the slip you use to pay money in the bank. It is also known as teller or deposit slip.

There was a company that had a fantastic manager who used to do well and was trusted by his employer. At a point, he changed and became dubious. He printed his own pay-in slip (deposit slip) just like a bank's and had his stamp on it. Instead of paying the money into the account, he used it for himself and submitted a fake teller. When the auditors reconciled the bank pay-in slip, they discovered the money in the pay-in slip did not reflect in the bank account. Eventually, they got to know that this man had been defrauding the company.

Whenever you send people to help you pay money into your account, please do not dispose of the deposit slip. It's a source document you need to file appropriately so that auditors can help you link up all these transactions together and lace it up. If the teller is a computer printout, do a photocopy or scan before you keep or before it fades.

Keep the entire source document mentioned because when auditors come, they will go through all of them to ensure you did things properly.

This knowledge of how to use source documents will help you prevent loss of the company's money.

Many businesses are not doing well because they lack knowledge, but this book has given you the knowledge about source document and other things that can help you grow your business.

## HOW TO CATEGORISE YOUR BUSINESS EXPENSES.

An auditor once rejected our books because we did not categorise our expenses and everything was a big mess. The only thing that made sense among all the documents we gave him were the bank statements.

I thought to myself; *We recorded every transaction inside the notebook without categorisation. I didn't know that there was a way to record our expenses.*

Categorisation involves classifying your expenses under various appropriate heads. For example, you can classify everything relating to purchase of pen, paper, ink, correcting fluid, etc., as stationeries.

Categorising your expenses makes it informative and organised. You will also be able to use it to decide as a business owner or an entrepreneur who is interested in his business's growth.

An expense in accounting is the money spent or cost incurred in an entity's effort to generate revenue while running the business.

What are the daily expenses you incur in your business? Some other examples are:

Electricity: includes government-supplied electricity, solar, or generator. When you use your generators, you will need to service them and buy one part at one time or the other; these expenses keep recurring.

You can have the breakdown in your petty cash account, e.g., filter XYZ amount, engine ABC, generator mechanic service, etc., but the breakdown should not pass the petty cash account while the total of those amount goes into the income and expenditure account. Just ensure that the breakdown is summed up into one so that you can easily know the total amount you spent servicing electricity or making sure that there is an alternative power supply in your business.

The reason for categorisation mainly is for you to critically analyse, review, evaluate transactions, and make meaningful decisions from them.

For those who are caterers, you can have pineapple flavour, apple flavour of xyz bottles, but when it's coming into the income and expenses account, it will just come in as *flavour* or *flavouring* only. This helps you to know the amount you spend on flavour per month and if there is a drastic increase in any month. That way, you will be able to ask questions.

If a hospital owner buys food for myself and other workers who are working late in the hospital, the food will reflect in my expense account as entertainment but for a caterer, it is a major expense in his business. For a caterer, rice can stand as an item but not so in a hospital's expense account.

You can compare from month to month to know when you are doing well because people who work for you may outsmart you if you don't have this clear categorisation and understanding of account in your business.

When you ask questions, your employees will respect you because they will understand that you are on top of the game. Unfortunately, many business owners usually agree with whatever they tell them until they eat deep into the company and realise that everything is gone.

We need to also teach our workers so that when they are submitting their feedback, they will know how to categorise these things which will help you judge easily what each money was used for.

## Chapter Twelve

# MIND YOUR FINANCES: TAXES

Tax is the money paid to the government other than for transaction of specific goods and services. It's a mandatory levy backed by law to be paid to the government.

There are various taxes specified by different countries to different categories of businesses. The taxes discussed below comply with Nigeria's financial act 2020. Find out what is obtainable in your country from a professional accountant or auditor.

Value Added Tax (VAT) is a tax levied on the price of product or services at each stage of production, distribution, or sales to the end consumer. An entrepreneur does not pay VAT, but the government collects it from consumers through the business.

Three categories of VAT are: VATable goods and services, VAT exempted, and Zero VAT.

Before paying any tax, you need to find out where your sector belongs. Zero VAT are lists of goods and services that are exempted from paying VAT and do not require VAT report, VAT exempted are lists of goods and services that are exempted from paying VAT but require monthly VAT report, while VATable goods and services are goods and services that require paying and reporting VAT monthly. Please note that there is a sanction for not paying and/or filing your report at the right time, monthly.

In Nigeria, VATable goods and services include, but not limited to, jewelries, shoes, bags, television, etc. All services rendered by a person in Nigeria, except those specifically exempted under the law, are VATable.

Small businesses are exempted from taking and paying VAT. Examples of VATable services are; services rendered by lawyers, engineers, accountants, contractors and consultants, etc.

## GOODS EXEMPTED

These are all pharmaceutical products, basic food items, books and educational materials, baby products, fertilizers, locally produced agricultural and veterinary medicine, farming machineries (tractors, ploughs, transportation equipment, all exporting slant and machineries imported for use in the Export Processing Zone), plant, machineries, and equipment purchased for utilisation of gas in downstream petroleum operations.

## SERVICES EXEMPTED

These are medical services, services rendered by community and people's banks, services rendered by mortgage institutions, plays and performances conducted by educational institutions as part of learning, and all export services. Note also: Exports are zero rated.

## EXEMPTED GOODS/SERVICES

If you sell goods or services that are exempted, you don't charge VAT. Small businesses in this category having below twenty-five million naira turnover are exempted while businesses with about twenty-five naira turnover will not pay VAT but will report monthly.

## ZERO-RATED GOODS

If you sell zero-rated goods or services, they count as taxable supplies. As a result of this, you don't add any VAT to your selling price because the VAT rate is 0 per cent. Thus, while no VAT is charged on providing goods and services taxable at zero-rate of VAT, you can still deduct VAT on costs and expenses you incur in making zero-rated supplies. Examples are:

1) All non-oil exports.
2) Goods and services purchased by diplomats.
3) Goods and services purchased for humanitarian donor funded projects.

A taxable person shall, within six (6) months of commencement of business, register his Tax Identification Number (TIN). Delay may attract sanctions (applicable in Nigeria) but you need to find out what is acceptable in your country.

Examples of books to keep are cashbook, accounts payable and receivables, inventory records, and records of your workers—indirect and direct labour.

Every business owner needs to know the laws of the land that govern businesses.

## Financial Acts 2020 And Modifications to the Value Added Tax Order Done In 2020.

In 2019, we heard of the finance bill—a document put together which brought about several changes to Nigerian tax laws. It got passed into law in 2020 and all amendments took shape on 3rd of February, 2020 but many business owners were not aware of it, which led to fines and sanctions that caused businesses to fail because of the inability to meet up.

For you to comply with your tax obligations, you must have a Tax payers Identification Number (TIN). I got mine six months late but was fined for the lateness which made me pay for something I should have gotten for free.

## Significance of the New Financial Act to Businesses and Categorisation Based on Annual Turnover.

| COMPANY CATEGORY | TURNOVER | CIT | VAT |
|---|---|---|---|
| SMALL | BELOW 25M | 0% | NO |
| MEDIUM | 25M - BELOW 100M | 20% | YES |
| LARGE | 100M ABOVE | 30% | YES |

| Company Category | Turnover | CIT | VAT |
|---|---|---|---|
| Small | Below 25M | 0% | No |
| Medium | 25M- Below 100M | 20% | Yes |
| Large | 100M Above | 30% | Yes |

The implication of this categorisation or financial act is that at the end of the year, financial profit for small businesses will not pay company income tax to the tax agencies; Federal Inland Revenue Service (FIRS).

Also, you will not charge your client for VAT. This is to encourage small businesses to improve the ease of doing business.

The medium category pays 20% of their profit as company income tax and also VAT.

Large businesses pay 30% of their profit as company income tax and also VAT.

VAT used to be 5% but now 7.5% of whatever you sell, provided that the goods or services are

VATable but if your turnover is below 25 million naira, you won't pay VAT.

### Value Added TAX (VAT)

This is a tax that is imposed on the supply of goods and services. If you buy a VATable product, the VAT will definitely be added to your receipt.

As at 3rd of February 2020, there was a new tax law which stated that VATable goods should be charged at 7.5% of the value. This means that if a product costs ₦100, you should add a ₦7.50, which a customer pays, but belongs to the government.

All taxable persons are required to file VAT monthly returns not later than the 21st day of the following month. For instance, you must pay your file VAT for the previous month between 21st of that month (previous month) and 21st of the current month, else you're going to pay a fine.

Three categories are supposed to pay VAT under the Nigerian law: Nigerian companies that are into VATable goods and services, government agencies parastatals and bodies, and oil companies. Before you start a business, you need to find out what category the goods and services fall under VAT (VATable, VAT

Exempted, and Zero VAT).

Sometimes, if you let a consumer know that you're charging them for VAT, they may not want to buy from you. As a result of this, you can sum it up in the total amount you're going to charge your customer to cover up for the 7.5% you will remit monthly to the government when you're filing for the VAT on or before 21st of the following month.

Some examples of VAT exemptions are item for babies from 0 to 3 years, basic food items, car utilisation, educational books and materials, electronic books, maps, music or religious books, transportation for public use but VIP transportation are taxable, residential rent by individuals while that of companies are taxable, petroleum products like aviation fuel and hydrocarbon gas for our cooking, motor spirit, kerosene gas, renewable energy (wind and solar), medical products and services, and downstream gas utilisation.

Tax is not optional. It's a compulsory contribution regardless of whether things are working in your country or not. I like when business owners see tax as their responsibility to where they live. Even a child has a responsibility to assist his parents at home. It can be as little as doing house chores.

If we see TAX payment as our responsibility, it makes things easier to do. Even if you think the money is not used for the right thing, yours is to do your best.

When some laws that are not conducive comes up, the best thing to do is to write to the house of the law so that they will pass another law that will negate them.

Tax is a compulsory contribution to the government levied by it on workers' income (pay as you earn), business's profit (company income tax), or VAT you pay on the cost of goods and services.

Basically, taxes are grouped into two.

## TYPES OF TAX

- Direct tax
- Indirect tax

## PAY AS YOU EARN

Their kind of tax is called PAYE. In Nigeria, all your full-time employees must pay their taxes.

When the law was passed in the state where my hospital is located, we wrote a letter to the tax agencies that we will oblige, but they should give us some time to explain to our employees. Fortunately, they granted our request.

We waited for the next staff meeting and discussed with the employees so that they can know ahead. For our new employees, we already informed them at the point of interview and by the time they got their employment letter, it was stated there.

In Kwara State, we also have some taxes like water rate and development levies, which are like ₦100 in a year.

Following the new finance act, all employees earning below ₦30,000 are exempted from paying tax, however, employees earning above that range are to pay taxes based on certain percentages.

For example, if someone earns ₦100,000 per month, you will multiply it by 12 to give ₦1,200,000 and take 20% out of it to give ₦240,000. You will add a constant amount of ₦200,000 to the ₦240,000 which equals ₦440,000. This is the amount allowable for you not to pay tax on. The remaining ₦760,000 is the amount taxable.

Amount taxable = ₦760,000

Amount allowable = ₦440,000

The first ₦300,000 of the amount taxable (₦760,000) will be charged at 7% giving ₦21,000.

₦760,000 − ₦300,000 = ₦460,000

Out of the remaining ₦460,000, another ₦300,000 will be charged at 11% giving ₦33,000

Afterwards, the remaining ₦160,000 will be charged at 15% giving ₦24,000. That makes the end of the charges. After calculating the charges, add all to obtain ₦78,000 (₦21,000+₦33,000+₦24,000 = ₦78,000).

Therefore, whoever earns ₦100,000 will pay a tax of ₦78,000 in a year which will be divided by 12. That gives a monthly tax payment of ₦6,500.

You, as a business owner, need to know this so that you can explain to your staff.

### PAYE OF ₦35000 can be calculated thus:

₦ 35,000*12 = ₦420,000

20% of ₦420,000 = ₦84,000

₦84,000+₦200,000 = ₦284,000 (Amount allowable)

₦420,000 − ₦284,000 = ₦136,000

### PAYE deduction:

7% of ₦136,000 = ₦9520 (tax payable per annum)
₦9520/12 = ₦793.33 (tax payable per annum)
₦793.33 + ₦150 (water rate) + ₦8.3 (development levy) = ₦951.63 (total PAYE)

## PERSONAL INCOME TAX (PIT)

Personal Income Tax (PIT) is an imposed tax on an individual who is running a business under a business name or partnership. Every business you have is an entity on its own and you have to pay personal income tax on it. This is a federal responsibility and it is generally collected by the state government.

FIRS collects it only from the residence of the Federal Capital Territory. Highly mobile federal workers also pay their taxes there.

PIT is paid on wages, salaries, bonuses, allowances, compensations, pensions, businesses, premiums, business income, percentage ownership, rent, fees, commission, interests, and dividends.

## TAX RELIEF

This is a way of reducing the amount of tax payable by an individual through tax cut. The degree of tax relief is always stated by the government or law.

Examples of reliefs are 5% paid on your national health insurance, 8% national pension fund, dividends and interest from quoted companies where you buy stocks from, rent and business expenses, etc.

You are allowed to do all your business expenses before you declare profit and pay your taxes.

The government also made an allowance that you should remove 20% of your annual income like that of PAYE, add ₦200,000 to it, and tax the rest.

### HOW TO CALCULATE YOUR PIT

Income taxes are calculated annually. If your total income is ₦3,000,000, your statutory relief is ₦800,000

20% of ₦3,000,000 = ₦600,000

₦600,000 + a constant of ₦200,000 = ₦800,000 (statutory relief).

You'll also remove 8% of the national pension fund and 2.5% of NHF (National Housing Fund) = ₦213,461.65k

₦213,461.65k + ₦800,000 = ₦1,013,461.65k

(tax relief from the government).

₦3,000,000 − ₦1,013,461.65 = ₦1,986,538.35k (taxable income)

To calculate your tax on taxable income, tax the first ₦300,000 at 7% = ₦21,000, and the second ₦300,000 at 11% = ₦33,000

Afterwards, tax the next ₦500,000 at 15% = ₦75,000 and another ₦500,000 at 19% = ₦95,000

21% of the balance: ₦386,538.35k at 21% = ₦81,173.05k

₦ (21,000+33,000+75,000+95,000+81,173.05) = ₦305,173.05 (Annual tax payable).

See links below for more details: https://www.yemisiadeyeye.com/blog/simplest-way-to-calculate-your-personal-income-tax-pit-1 hpps.firs.gov.ng

## WITHHOLDING TAX

This is a method used to collect income tax in advance. It means the government wants to get taxes from you in advance. Anytime anyone supplies you something, you are supposed to withhold a tax of 5-10% from it, depending on the transaction, and you are going to give the person some note to prove that.

This money has to be remitted on the 21st day of every month. The penalty for late payment is ₦25,000 for the first month, and ₦5,000 for each subsequent months the failure continues.

All organisations making payments to suppliers of goods and services are required to make deductions of withholding tax and remit to the tax authorities as payment are being made to suppliers and vendors. It will be paid on behalf of that company (supplier) to the tax authority. At the end of the year, the tax paid in advance will be deducted by the supplier from the annual payment.

# Conclusion

Congratulations on reading *Entrepreneurship Is A Beautiful Thing*. This is a business guide effective at turning your business into an organisation with the use of systems and controls and you have learnt a lot about the different aspects of a business. You are skilled at what you do, either manufacturing products or rendering services; but this book would help you with business management aspect that many business owners struggle with.

So far, I have exposed you to the basic steps, strategies, tools, and knowledge in running a business in an organised way. You have also learnt how to put structures that bring peace of mind in your business. Finally, you have learnt how to create systems in your venture and turn it into an organisation that will last for a long time.

By practising all you have learnt in this book,

you can take the much-needed vacation, spend time with loved ones, focus on your personal development or other businesses, and still have your present business running smoothly.

As a business management consultant and a multiple award-winning, practising entrepreneur running a successful and thriving business in Nigeria, I have used my experience, education, and expertise in writing this book, which is relevant across different sectors.

As your relatable business teacher, I ensured I neither made any assumption on the level of knowledge you are in the journey of entrepreneurship, nor did I focus on the healthcare sector where I operate.

As business principles are useful across many business sectors, I broke down major areas that needed in-depth explanations like *Fundamentals of Entrepreneurship*, my model (*Yemisi Adeyeye's Entrepreneurship Model*) which makes business run smoothly, profitably, and sustainably, *Legal Business Entities* (business registration matters), *Human Resource Management* (how to manage your employees), *Customer Relationship Management* (how to keep your customers coming back to you), *Sources of Funding For Businesses* (how to get more funding for your business), *Bookkeeping, Accounting,* and *Tax.*

Indeed, this book is loaded and I am very sure you can attest to that, too.

I expect you will put the needed structures into your business and document your company's policies, processes, and procedures right away. Do not stop until you achieve the business of your dream. If you need help in achieving this, feel free to send me your questions, suggestions, or feedback and interact with me via:

www.yemisiadeyeye.com

hello@yemisiadeyeye.com

adeyeye.yemisi@yahoo.com

Instagram: @yemisiadeyeye

WhatsApp: +234-909-440-7502

Your company's HR policy manual helps each staff to know exactly what to do per time and the sanctions for defaulters. Managing your staff is a lot easier when your company's rules and regulations are well documented.

To get templates you can easily use to create or customise your company's HR policies, visit www.yemisiadeyeye.com/hrtemplate

I look forward to seeing you develop giant strides in your business.

Entrepreneurship Is A Beautiful thing....

...the guide book for every seasoned, aspiring, and budding business owner to run a successful and sustainable business with peace of mind.

www.ingramcontent.com/pod-product-compliance
Lightning Source LLC
Chambersburg PA
CBHW060823220526
45466CB00003B/959